In Search of the Painted Bunting

Praise for *In Search of the Painted Bunting*

In Search of the Painted Bunting: (Mis)Adventures of a Birdwatching Family is a humorous chronicle of an extended family bouncing around the back roads of America in rented twelve-passenger vans. Eldon N. Spady is the author, ringleader, and driver of the various vans in the family's true adventures.

Spady addresses seven trips taken by his family of bird lovers and, in the process, he provides useful information, directions to state parks, Audubon areas, preserves, and, believe it or not, people's homes, where their gardens or feeders have become renowned on the bird circuit as productive places to stop and watch.

Most of the adventures are American road trips—via rental vans and inexpensive motels—but the family's trip to Costa Rica breaks the mold of the commonplace with a packaged expedition that caters to birders by pampering them with guides, good food, and elegant lodging. Spady makes the point that the business of tourism has recognized the potential of bird watching as an economic activity.

Each chapter that recounts the misadventures of a particular trip concludes with a list of birds seen on the tour. The lists are not slight, and at the end of the book, Spady has included a consolidated look at sightings amounting to a full six and a half double-columned pages.

In Search of the Painted Bunting is a lighthearted and light-handed book with an undercurrent of handy data for the birder. As Spady says, "Everyone defines fun in his or her own way, but for me and my family, fun is the result of getting together and spending time being ourselves. In our case, birding is our excuse."

—Pete Warzel,
Clarion Review

Eldon Spady's humorous tales of his family's birding adventures gave me a bird's-eye view (pun intended) of how avid birdwatchers stalk their prey. *In Search of the Painted Bunting* made me want to go on a birding expedition myself! Spady's quirky sense of humor makes for an entertaining read as he tells us about the "worm-eating warbler salute" and the "Spanish-crowing Mexican crow," and that "viewed through tinted windows, every bird is a blackbird." There's plenty of serious birdwatching between the covers, often punctuated by generous helpings of family fun. From Spady's book on management—*The No-Drama Manager*—I know how a little gentle fun-poking can add value to relationships.

—Taylor Townes, CFP
Vice President—Investments

In Search of the Painted Bunting

(MIS)ADVENTURES OF A BIRDWATCHING FAMILY

Eldon N. Spady

CREATESPACE

In Search of the Painted Bunting

(Mis)adventures of a Birdwatching Family

Edited by Robin McBride
Cover art by Debbie Hosier
Cover and interior design by RMcB Creative Services

ISBN 978-1482583397

LCCN 2013908683

Printed in U.S.A. by CreateSpace

Table of Contents

I'd like to dedicate this book to the people who made it possible—especially those who accompanied me on these adventures and have the physical, emotional, and psychological scars to prove it—although I'm not sure how many of the psychological scars are directly due to traveling with me. We'll just assume that all their comments about the effects of my driving on their mental health are somewhat overstated.

There is Lorraine, my wife and companion on all these treks, as well as the ace bird-identifier and faithful keeper of the birds-sighted list.

There are my brother Ken Spady and his wife Irene along with my sister Dorothy and her husband Ted Naiman. Then there is nephew Steve Spady, his wife Angie, and Steve's son Tyler.

Included in this intrepid group is, of course, our granddaughter Haley Stinson and Angie's daughter Channing Everage.

Also a big part of making this manuscript readable is Robin McBride who used her editing and typesetting skills to great advantage and Karla McMechan who proofread this manuscript to make sure that we were not stepping on our own feet. Debbie Hosier used her artistic talents to create the cartoon which appears on the cover.

All these people together made it possible to bring forth the book you hold in your hands, and for that I tender my sincere thanks.

—Eldon N. Spady

Preface

Birdwatching—excuse me, birding—is one of the fastest-growing leisure-time activities in America, or so I've been told (come to think of it, by other birders who probably hope that there may be sanity in numbers).

What makes birding so popular? Among other things, it's fun.

Many state tourist bureaus have taken advantage of this trend by establishing organized "birding trails" (not actual trails in most cases) in their states, publishing maps, and advertising them on the internet, in magazines, or anyplace else they feel they might catch a birder's eye.

If only one nuthatch has been seen by some lake somewhere, this lake is added to the system of that state's birding trails. Birds seem to avoid some states altogether, but we'll talk about that later.

It takes little effort for states to designate birding trails. They just tell birders that if you drive here or hike there or stop alongside a certain road or trail and look in that direction, you *may* see birds cavorting about. As you can imagine, it's a safe bet. Everyone understands the flightiness of birds.

The states do this because they've become aware of birders wandering around other states spending money—lots of money. So each state thinks, "Why not in our state?"

The Family That Birds Together . . .

In the following pages you will meet some members of my family who take trips together, not only to enjoy birding, but to use it as an excuse to carve out time from busy schedules to get together and have some fun. Our travel experiences may not be typical—we can only hope—but they *are* true and could certainly happen to you. At any rate, our birding is not just about the birds. It's about a far-flung family that gets a kick out of spending time together.

Cast of Characters, and I Do Mean "Characters"

To avoid reader confusion, let me introduce the people involved in these trips up front.

Eldon and Lorraine

I'm Eldon and, well, the less said the better. I travel with Lorraine, who, as luck would have it, is my wife. That's lucky on several levels, not the least of which is, considering the travel arrangements, I would have trouble explaining these trips if she *weren't* my wife. During the span of the trips covered by this book, Lorraine and I lived in Texas, Wisconsin, and Kentucky. (We're not really itinerant gypsies. My work takes me to different locales.)

Ken and Irene, Steve, Angie, and Tyler

Ken is my older brother. I have to say older because when people see us together they have trouble telling which of us is the younger, a great argument for living a clean and upstanding life. Then there is Ken's wife Irene, Ken's son Steve, Steve's wife Angie, and Steve's son Tyler. Ken and Irene live in Washington state. Steve, Angie, and Tyler live in Kentucky.

Dorothy and Ted

Dorothy is my sister, which makes Ted, her husband, my brother-in-law. They split their time between West Virginia and Colorado.

Channing and Haley

You'll meet these two young ladies, Channing and Haley, in Chapter Six.

Let me throw in a few more details here concerning these people. Both Ken and Steve are medical doctors. Dorothy is a nurse. Ted has had a long, health-related, career, teaching for many years at the National Mine Health and Safety Academy and more recently being responsible, among other things, for the correct disposal of all medical waste at a large Eastern university medical center. Both Irene and Lorraine worked for years supervising the paperwork in medical clinics, and Angie is a representative for a pharmaceutical company.

So for anything that might go wrong medically speaking, we're set. Our group contains three people to take care of us, a person to dispose of any body parts that might have to be abandoned, someone to provide substances to make us feel better about it, and two to handle the paperwork. It's a great team!

Chapter One

Barely North of the Border

It was a hot Texas May morning when Lorraine and I caught an early flight to Tucson. We were met at the airport by Ken, Irene, Tyler, and Steve, who had rented a real van this year. Not a mini like we used last year, but an eleven-passenger thing that seemed about half a block long. It contained enough seating that each seat only had to hold two people, leaving a back seat just for equipment and baggage. It was a nice setup. I was elected to drive. I climbed into the driver's seat and headed us south toward Madera Canyon. Of course everyone was looking for birds before we even got out of the airport parking lot. After all, wasn't that the official excuse for this family gathering?

Birding in Southeastern Arizona

You're probably asking yourself "Why Arizona?" and "Why would they do this in May instead of, like, February?" The answer to the first question is easy. Southeastern Arizona is one of the great birding areas in the United States. This portion of Arizona is where the Sierra Madre of Mexico, the Sonoran and Chihuahuan deserts, and several small mountain ranges all converge, creating very diverse habitats. It is especially well-known for its hummingbirds.

"Why would we do this in May?" is a little harder. Suffice it to say that Steve had gotten the idea in his head that May was a really hot birding time. No pun intended. It was hot all right, but just think—we could have gone in August.

First Stop Madera Canyon

We headed south out of Tucson on Highway 19 and turned east toward Madera Canyon. The moment we approached the mouth of the canyon, we started to see birds. Madera Canyon is a slash in the northern face of the Santa Rita Mountains. It's great bird habitat.

By the time we came to the end of the canyon road, the group was hungry, so we decided to have some lunch before exploring our surroundings. (As you read on, you will begin to see a pattern here.) Luckily, we found a nice picnic area there for people just like us. By that I mean other people who are hungry—not that other people are anything like us. I'm not trying to insult anyone. The moment we got our food spread out on a table, what should appear but a number of Acorn Woodpeckers. They seemed to be partial to cheese puffs (ain't we all?). The Acorn Woodpecker is a rather striking bird. Along with a bright red cap, it has very distinct black and white markings and white eye rings, which give it a look of being perpetually surprised.

After lunch we hiked a couple miles up one of the trails into the canyon. Now the main area of the canyon is at about five thousand feet. The picnic area is up from that, and the trail goes up from the picnic area. This may not seem like much to ya'll, but for us flatlanders five thousand plus seemed high. That's the only thing I have to say about all the huffing, puffing, and wheezing as we hiked up the trail. Luckily we had occasional clouds along with an occasional breeze, but when the sun peeked out it was blistering.

Part of the time the trail followed a small stream, and the whole way we were beating the bushes for unsuspecting birds. We saw several, but to our disappointment not the Elegant Trogon that was reputed to dwell in these parts. Along the trail we kept meeting people who claimed with straight faces that the Elegant Trogons were, in fact, on the other trail leading out of the parking lot; or that they had seen several dozen down by the gift shop and cabins; or they'd been forced to shoo them off their car before they could open the doors to get out. Again a recurring theme in this book, as the reader will learn. No one had seen trogons where we were. That's pretty much how the whole trip went. Everything we wanted to see always seemed to be just over the next ridge, back a couple miles, or in the next canyon. It became one of our many running jokes, but luckily, there were several major exceptions to this trend.

We finally returned to the van and drove back down to the main part of the canyon where there were some cabins and a gift shop, all part of the Santa Rita Lodge. The lodge owners had put out many feeders for hummingbirds and any other birds that might be hungry. Along with the feeders there were benches where people could relax while observing the birds. We saw plenty of hummers, jays, and more Acorn Woodpeckers. Watching Acorn Woodpeckers trying to drink out of hummingbird feeders was like going to the bird circus. But they succeeded!

By this time, the afternoon was waning so we decided to head toward the small town of Patagonia, where we planned to spend the night. As we were exiting the parking lot, an Acorn Woodpecker landed right in front of the van. Surely it would fly up at the last minute, I thought, just about the time I felt a bump under the wheel. I had run over the woodpecker! Well, I didn't do it personally, but one of the van tires sure did. We backed up to make sure it wasn't suffering or maybe in need of medical attention. (Remember, we had two doctors along and I assumed the Hippocratic Oath also covers woodpeckers.) Steve jumped out to see if it might be stuffable road kill. Believe me, it wasn't. When Steve says "stuffable" he is not thinking of stuffing as in turkey and Thanksgiving. He means taxidermy. We all felt so much better when he made that clear.

As I drove away I was barraged with comments about my reflexes, my eyesight, my callous attitude concerning wildlife, and my driving in general. At dinner that evening Ken commented, "It gave a whole new meaning to the term 'life list.'" I retorted with, "Well anybody can just mark them down!" The remarks just went downhill from there. After all, we came to have fun, right?

Back on Highway 19, we stopped in Green Valley, the nearest town to the mouth of the canyon, to get an Arizona State road map (the collective intelligence had finally concluded that one might come in handy) and find a place to eat some dinner (eating—that recurring theme again). Along with the map we got directions to several eating places, only one of which we trusted to serve us what turned out to be good TexMex food.

Patagonia

We arrived in Patagonia after it was too dark to see what we were doing. We had made lodging reservations ahead of time at the Stage Stop Inn. Over the years this inn has served as the working headquarters for several movie and TV filming crews. It has a lot of character. The pool looked inviting until we got close enough to see unidentifiable gunk floating all over the surface of the water. That, added to our inability to see the bottom of the pool, sort of cooled us on the idea of cooling ourselves with a swim.

By 6:15 the next morning, we were up and on our way again. Our first stop was the Nature Conservancy's Patagonia-Sonoita Creek Preserve, a lovely riparian area criss-crossed with walking trails. It boasts a great diversity of plant life, and we were able to spot a number of birds. Along the creek bed grew the largest cottonwood trees I've ever seen. Some are a good ten feet in diameter, very tall and beautiful, and reported to be up to 130 years old. In addition to the riparian grasses and shrubs, there were cactus, but the area did not have the typical Sonoran-desert look generally associated with southern Arizona.

Along the trail we met several people, one of whom was a gentleman with one eye that looked off to his left at the same time his other eye looked straight at you. A hard-core birder, he was very knowledgeable. We exchanged information about what we had all seen so far. Then, before he left, he told us how to find a Rose-throated Becard's nest at the rest stop out on the highway from Patagonia to Nogales. The thing particularly unique about a Rose-throated Becard is that it's primarily a bird of Mexico. The bird itself has a light-gray underside, dark gray on the head and back, and a rose-colored throat—hence the name. This little corner of Arizona and the area around Brownsville, Texas, are the only places in the United States to see one.

The Patons, a couple who once lived in this part of Arizona, placed numerous hummingbird feeders in their backyard, which they opened to any and all who came to watch the birds. At any given time there could be thirty to fifty hummingbirds sipping nectar or buzzing around. They had even set up an awning with chairs under it to shade birders from the sun—a very comfortable arrangement. The Paton's place and their hospitality have been written about in just about every birding guide to southwestern Arizona. Their generosity has been appreciated by thousands of birders from all over the country. They are now deceased, but interested parties continue to maintain the place.

However, when we got there, the gate was locked. We couldn't get into their yard. Rather than knock down the fence, we decided to go back to the inn for some breakfast and to check out. We ordered and, after a long wait, the waitress returned and admitted to us that she had a new chef in the kitchen. When the food finally came, every order was garbled in some way. Most of us got more than we ordered or needed, because of their efforts to get it all right.

As we ate, we got to talking about our new, sight-advantaged acquaintance and the multitude of possible advantages there might be for a birder who could see in two directions

at once. That led us to other unrelated topics which created a certain amount of mirth. Fortunately the restaurant was nearly empty. The only other patron finally took her breakfast out by the pool. It was really nice out there, so I'm sure her choice had nothing to do with us and our noisy levity.

After breakfast we tried the Patton's place again. Before leaving, Steve said that he needed to "go and, ah, make a phone call." Later, when we found him, it was clear he had found a unique, dual-purpose, phone booth. When he said the call had made him feel like a king, we didn't ask any questions. This time we found the gate unlocked. Who should we find there but our sight-advantaged friend, working his long camera lens on the hummingbirds.

True birders can't get within a half mile of another birder without striking up a conversation about what they should be seeing, what they have seen, what they have heard someone else has seen, what they heard that someone heard that someone saw, what the latest birding magazine said should be seen in this spot (and by spot I don't mean in this part of Arizona, but this *very* spot wherever that may be), and whether "*Birds Are Us*" magazine is better than "*Birder's Universe.*" You get the picture. As we made the circuit of southeastern Arizona, we kept running into the same people so often that we now know some of them by their first names and will probably get several invitations for Thanksgiving dinner.

Heading out of Patagonia, we followed the previous day's directions to the becard's nest. We finally found the fabled rest stop after we gave up looking for the kind of rest area we would see in a more civilized part of the country. It was a dirt turn-out with no facilities whatsoever. Following the directions, we crossed the road and got lost almost immediately. Not that we didn't know where we were, but nothing looked like the directions, which said nothing about the fence immediately in front of us or the river just beyond the fence, both of which seemed rather prominent features in this particular landscape. We were dashing about trying to find something that resembled the directions, when our direction-giving friend arrived. He cast around for a while, finally locating the right tree, and sure enough, we saw our first Rose-throated Becard.

Ramsey Canyon

It was so hot by this time that we left our friend trying to call up some Thick-billed Kingbirds (I'm not just making up these names) with his portable audio system and drove east on Highway 82 to catch Highway 90 down past Sierra Vista to Ramsey Canyon—another Nature Conservancy preserve.

Let me say something here about Nature Conservancy. Instead of complaining about what other people are doing with their own land, this organization buys, or has donated to them, land they feel offers something worth protecting. They then make that land available for the public to enjoy. The Conservancy manages the property in conjunction with the original landowner, the Forest Service, or whoever else it can get to help. To my way of thinking, it's a fine and admirable way to protect unique places.

In Ramsey Canyon we walked the "red" nature trail and went a little way up the "green" trail, even though we only had "red" trail passes. This is a no-no. To help limit the impact on the canyon, the Conservancy issues passes for certain trails. One being a red pass for—guess what?—the red trail, and so forth.

We saw some birds and our first coati. The coati, for those of you who are not familiar with this exotic creature, looks much like a large raccoon, except that its tail and snout are longer and the tail is not as distinctly ringed with dark circles. The one we saw was larger than a raccoon and had a black nose, a long white snout, and white rings around the eyes with a sort of dark mask around the white rings. Come to think of it, the only thing that reminded us of a raccoon was that it had four legs and a bushy tail. One thing for sure, it didn't look like a cow.

The Conservancy also had a hummingbird feeding station where we saw our first Anna's Hummingbird. A couple of other gentlemen had their scopes set up and, like most birders, they invited us to share the use of them. We were able to see the birds as if they were in our hands. The bright sun made their coloring look unreal. The male Anna's has a very distinct deep-rose-red head and throat. The gentlemen sharing their scopes tried to convince us that one of the birds we were seeing was a Costa's Hummingbird, but Steve gently nailed them up against the proverbial bird-book wall, so to speak. Steve soon got a reputation in that part of Arizona for straightening people out on identifications.

By the end of the trip, any time there was a group around, no one wanted to offer an opinion without getting the nod from the tall, balding, blond guy with the dead woodpecker hanging out of his back pocket. (Okay, maybe it wasn't quite that bad, but it was close).

As the trip progressed we each fell into our natural role. Lorraine kept track of what we saw and helped with identification. I drove the van and spotted birds. Tyler's young eyes made him an excellent spotter. Steve was also a good spotter and knew his birds. Irene made sure we didn't miss any meals, and Ken had the patience to notice, for example, that it was the third secondary (wing feather) that was a slightly lighter shade of brown, to help nail down the identifications.

Portal and the Chiricahua Wilderness

Leaving Ramsey Canyon, we aimed ourselves toward the town of Portal, located another hundred miles east, close to the New Mexico border. The town and surrounding area is located close to the Chiricahua Wilderness. In fact the road to Portal crosses into New Mexico before turning back into Arizona. We were looking forward eagerly to what we could see in this near-wilderness area.

On the way to Portal we stopped in Douglas for some dinner. This town sits just barely north of the border between the U.S. and Mexico. As we eased through town looking for a likely eating place, we coasted up beside a fellow walking his bike along the street. Steve leaned out and asked, "Do you know any good places to eat around here?" The gentleman named a place that was famous for barbecue. Steve promptly informed him that we (*he*) didn't like barbecue. Then he told us about a good place for Chinese. Steve promptly replied that we (*he*) didn't want Chinese. By this time the bicyclist was trying to edge away from us like he needed to be somewhere else. As a parting shot, he gave us a string of directions to a Mexican eatery. We followed his directions to the letter and found nothing.

As a last resort Steve put the question to some folks in a convenience store who sent us to the No Name Café, which turned out to be right across the street from where we had encountered the cyclist in the first place. The decor consisted of many, many pictures of Marilyn Monroe on the walls, but this Hispanic family of restaurateurs, being obviously very religious, had also included one picture of Christ and one of the "Last Supper." The food was good despite the semi-nausea inspired by a peek into the kitchen as I walked back to the restrooms.

When we couldn't hold any more Mexican food, we drove for another hour and arrived in Portal. It was so dark we couldn't see where we were, but it certainly felt like the backside of beyond. With no artificial light, the stars looked very close, and we could smell the aroma of sage, juniper, and unmolested earth. It was great!

In the morning we found that we were really not as close to the end of the earth as we had thought the night before. However, if you stood up on the bumper of the van, you could see it.

The nearest town, Rodeo, New Mexico, was ten miles away. Its population numbered about 150 if you counted the chickens.

I had driven all day that day without running over anything except some mice on the highway after dark. The whole crew was proud of me, and perhaps just a little surprised after the woodpecker incident. Why they felt so compelled to keep making comments about their surprise was a little beyond me, but that's family for you.

Knowing we would arrive late, we had called ahead to Portal Peak Lodge. As everything closed down at 7:30 p.m., they just left our motel keys under the door mats. We were pleasantly surprised to find that the units assigned to us were new and nice.

We had debated what time to get going in the morning. Ken was pushing for 6:30 a.m. Reluctantly, he agreed to sleep in. Our mistake was in not defining "sleeping in." Guess who tapped on our doors at 5:30 the next morning? Sure enough, Ken was up and around and couldn't wait to be on the move.

When we emerged from our rooms and looked around, we found ourselves just outside the mouth of a large canyon flanked by massive rock formations. It was very beautiful in a rugged, rocky, sagebrushy sort of way. The town of Portal (some cabin/motel units, a little store/restaurant, a couple houses, post office, and library) is situated on the edge of one section of the Coronado National Forest, which in this area covers the Chiricahua Mountains, the homeland of the Chiricahua Apaches and not far from Cochise's Stronghold.

The birding possibilities in this area include Cave Creek Canyon itself, plus two separate hummingbird feeding stations—one at the ranger station and one at the Spoffords' private residence. Like the Patons in Patagonia, the Spoffords are another couple who had fixed up their backyard with bird feeders of all kinds and plenty of places to sit and observe. We spent two sessions there and several over at the ranger station. We did see several new birds between the two. Think about these Spoffords a minute. In their backyard, by their own design no less, there were from one to a couple dozen people at any one time all day long, looking toward the back of their house through binoculars. I'm guessing these good folks are so dedicated to birdwatching that privacy is of secondary importance to them. Their hospitality is enjoyed and appreciated by all comers.

As we headed over toward the ranger station, we saw a house back off the road a ways that was under construction.

The walls of the house seemed to be built of bales of straw. We drove in to check it out. And sure enough, they were. The roof was on, but the doors and windows were not yet in place. The walls had no siding on the outside, nor was there anything covering the bales on the inside. Just hay bales for walls! Before leaving the area we saw a couple other houses under construction using the same materials. It would sure rule out having a goat or a cow for a pet. I've since learned that the normal process is to cover the hay bales inside and out with stucco.

As we drove up the canyon, morning light lit up the rock walls. At its mouth the canyon is probably between one and two miles wide, but it looks a lot narrower because of the massive height of the canyon walls. The color and light were beautiful. We got some excellent photos.

Our mission on this particular day was to find an Elegant Trogon. Now I know that the audacity of this challenge must be taking your breath away, but remember we are talking about six very tough and intrepid people who care nothing for personal safety or comfort when in pursuit of something as elusive and exceptional as an Elegant Trogon.

Let me describe this spectacular bird. It has a dark face with green on top of its head and down its back. This green is iridescent in the right light. It also has this same green on its upper breast with a stripe of white below that, giving way to a bright red on the rest of its front down onto and partway under its tail. The rest of its undertail is white with fine black lines like oriental etching down to the black band across the end of the tail. The upper side of the tail is iridescent bronze down to the black band at the tip. The bird is about thirteen inches long—not a small thing. The beak is sort of a cross between those of a grosbeak and a parrot. That may not be the best description, but the best you're going to get from me. It would be worth your time to look it up.

We drove to the picnic area at the South Fork of Cave Creek and then took the trail up the canyon. We saw a number of birds, but no Elegant Trogons. After a bit we heard two trogons calling back and forth, but we couldn't see them. At this point the canyon walls were much closer together. Finally, as Steve gazed off into the distance at the far canyon wall a couple hundred yards away, he spotted one sitting on a tree about half way up the side of the canyon. He put Ken's scope on it, giving three of us a look before it flew away. The other three were disappointed and all the more determined to find one that we could see up close.

Another mile or so up the trail, we heard another trogon calling and tried to track it down. The canyon was quite narrow in this area, and we thought we might finally have a shot (so to speak). We scanned the trees on the canyon slopes, knowing from the sound that it had to be close. As five of us diligently searched, Irene, who was standing about fifty feet behind us on the trail asked, "Hey guys, what's that bird right above your heads?" Somewhat miffed that she wouldn't help track down our rare bird, we finally condescended to look straight up, and there sat an Elegant Trogon not more than thirty feet above us!

We watched until it flew to a lower branch off to the side of the trail about fifty feet away. We had a very good view. Ken focused his scope on the bird, and we all just stood there enjoying its beauty. A short distance to one side, another trogon came out of a hole in a tree trunk and flew off into the woods. "Our" trogon flew over and climbed into the hole. HOLY MOTHER OF BIRDWATCHERS! We not only had a trogon, but we had a trogon nest. I sat at the base of a nearby tree with my long lens zeroed in on the nest hole for about twenty minutes waiting for that trogon to reappear, but it never came out.

At this point we became the trogon experts of Portal, if not for that entire part of Arizona. As we headed back down the trail, we told everyone we met what we had seen and gave directions on how to get there. Thanks to Tyler, we even knew the number of paces from the creek crossing up to the nest. We tried to be casual about it as if we found trogons' nests every day. We would meet someone on the trail and ask them what they had seen. After telling us, they would then ask about our sightings. We would list everything except the trogon and then add as an afterthought, "Oh yeah, and then there was that pair of trogons and their nest...."

On the trail we ran into a husband and wife who were not carrying the usual birding equipment, which was rare in these parts. They asked what we had seen and when we started to tell them about bird sightings the fellow made it abundantly clear that he was looking for snakes, bears, mountain lions—manly stuff. They were friendly enough but just not interested in birds. The lady, by the way, had bright red hair. That will be important to remember as this thriller unfolds.

Full of our great trogon triumph, we drove back down to the ranger station to watch the hummingbirds again. As I pulled into the parking area I noticed a green Forest Service truck behind me with all its lights flashing. After eyeing the van suspiciously and easing up to the driver-side window, the ranger asked, "Are you a tour group?"

"No," I replied. "We're parts of a far-flung family that's joined forces to see your birds." This seemed to relax him some (clearly he didn't know anything about *this* family). He then kindly explained that I had been doing 35 in a 20 mph zone and that this speed limit applied throughout the entire park. At least the news of a gray van running over birds had apparently not yet reached him all the way from Madera Canyon. He seemed satisfied that I looked contrite enough and refrained from giving me a ticket. Of course this incident brought forth another round of derisive comments from the non-drivers in our group.

No sooner had the ranger left than our sight-advantaged friend from Patagonia pulled into the parking area. We took time to catch up on what everyone had seen in the last twelve hours. Somehow Irene had learned that this gentleman was a pediatrician from Phoenix. From then on we referred to him as "the Doctor." Now that we were friends, we found it easier not to be so envious of his seeing advantage.

We stopped at the store/restaurant for some lunch. Everyone of us ordered like a normal, civilized person until the waitress got to Steve. "I'd like a Reuben sandwich," he said. Sounds simple enough, doesn't it? But he went on. "I don't want any meat in it, and I want it on wheat bread instead of rye. And I want extra sauerkraut to take the place of the meat." The waitress, an older woman who had raised a couple of boys herself, took it in stride. It was good for a laugh, and they certainly knew who we were from that time on.

As soon as we finished lunch we drove out to Rodeo to tank up on gas, then back to Spofford's in Portal to check out the hummingbirds. As I mentioned before, you could see right into the house through the patio doors, and several windows, so their privacy was pretty limited. Why someone would put up with that was hard for me to understand, but I'm not what I would consider a hard-core birder. I mean, it's something I enjoy, but I don't get all twitchy if I can't do it for a while.

Like the Patons' home in Patagonia, Spoffords' property has been listed in every Arizona birder's guide written in the last twenty years. Their backyard and generosity have been appreciated by thousands of birders and, I'm sure, millions of birds.

After another short stop at the ranger station, we drove up the canyon to the Southwestern Research Center of the American Natural History Museum. We'd heard there were all kinds of unusual hummingbirds visiting their feeders. We settled down to watch the birds coming and going. Or some of us did. The problem with this location was that just beyond the bird-feeder area was the center's swimming pool. That late in the afternoon there were a number of center staff lounging around the pool, many of them bathing-suit-clad young ladies. Several of our group had difficulty focusing their equipment on the birds—*humming*birds, that is. They were roundly chastised by the more conscientious among us and promised to mend their ways. It's hard to make the promise sound sincere when you're squinting through a scope and salivating at the same time. You'll notice I haven't mentioned any names up to now. But, Ken and I both had our wives along, and our mamma didn't raise no fools.

It was getting late in the day and we had an appointment with an Elf Owl which was reported to leave its nest each evening between 7:24 and 7:42. The timing had nothing to do with the clock, but rather with the onset of dusk. While we were waiting, we made another quick pass around the South Fork Picnic Area looking for Strickland's Woodpeckers. Then, before heading out to see the owl, we stopped at the restaurant to pick up some take-out sandwiches, as the place would close before we got done with the owl—or the owl got done with us. In this back of Arizona's beyond, the locals believe no one has a legitimate reason to be out and about after dark unless they're looking at owls.

Earlier in the day we had located the owl tree, right across from the post office. When we arrived in the evening we found that the owl had changed residence in the past couple of hours, but it had only moved two trees down the road. A sizable group had gathered near the tree, all waiting to see the Elf Owl emerge.

As I've already mentioned, this owl comes out at dusk to change places with its mate; therefore the light is always marginal. Only about two-thirds the length of a robin and fourteen shades of brown, the owl *is* hard to see. Our doctor friend was there with his long lens and a spotlight so he could take some pictures. Sure enough, at around 7:25 this little owl stuck its head out of the nest hole and looked around. The Doctor turned on his spotlight, illuminating a good view of the little fellow. Twice he poked his head up, and twice we had a good look—as did the bird, I assume. The second time, a birding "nazi" (yes, they do exist just to set us all straight) approached the Doctor and demanded he douse his light, claiming it frightened the owl and would keep it from coming out. The fact that we had just had two good views thanks to his light seemed to escape her. Nevertheless, her admonition got some scattered applause from her traveling companions. The Doctor complied but explained to her that he had done this several times before without preventing the owl from exchanging places with its mate. Once again, the owl stuck its head out, looked around, and went back. Soon it climbed out of the nest and flew away. By then it was so dark we could only tell that something came out and left. We didn't really see it go. As we were all leaving, the birding nazis were standing around congratulating themselves on having straightened out yet another nature abuser.

Back at the lodge we sat around one of the deck tables eating our sandwiches while Ken and Steve related a few of the more bizarre medical situations they had encountered recently. Their stories left us all laughing so hard and loud I feared we might get kicked out of the place, but our neighbors seemed to take us in stride, evidently chalking it up to birders having fun.

One of those neighbors was a fellow who had been looking for "a little Japanese guy" (his description) for the past two days. They were supposed to be catching up and meeting somewhere. Every time we encountered this gentleman he would ask us again if we had seen the Japanese man yet. Then we started seeing the Japanese gentleman all over the place, but he never looked as though he had missed anybody. We made no effort to get them together as it didn't appear that the look*ee* was at all interested in meeting up with the look*er*. We only spoke to the Japanese gentleman one time, when Steve sorted him out about misidentifying a bird.

We started the next day by driving up out of the canyon to Rustler Park, about fifteen miles up a narrow, graveled, twisty road, with views out over the surrounding mountains stretching into Mexico. The park features a large meadow, surrounded by big pines and firs, with lots of open space for camping and picnicking. It's at an elevation of about 8,500 feet. Rustlers used the meadow for hiding stolen cattle while the altered brands were healing; they also parked their horses there while doing something other than riding.

We followed a trail up out of the meadow to a lookout station situated atop a nearby peak about one and a half miles away. Along the trail, who should we catch up with but our red-headed lady acquaintance and her husband, whose names were Betty and Pat. Pat had had zippo luck finding his manly wildlife. They walked with us for a while, even deigning to look at a few birds with us, quite tickled when they could spot something before we did. We reached the top, rested for a while, talked a bit with the resident ranger, and then started back down the trail. We again caught up with Betty and Pat, who told us about a bird they had spotted and wanted some help identifying. They kept pace with us for a while before we gradually pulled ahead of them after telling them how to find the trogon's nest.

On our way back down to Portal, we stopped at the South Fork Picnic Area again, where Steve, Lorraine, and I got dropped off so we could once more hike up to the trogon's nest. We were hoping to get some pictures.

Because Portal Peak Lodge was completely booked for a third night, we had made reservations at nearby Cave Creek Ranch. Steve and I had already popped in to make sure the reservations were confirmed, but we hadn't really checked out the accommodations. The place looked a little scummy, but we had resigned ourselves to our fate, as there was no other place to stay in Portal. At this point Ken, Irene, and Tyler went on down to check us in.

Before leaving the South Fork parking lot, Steve, Lorraine, and I got to talking with two guys—father and son, Tom and John, respectively—who were also there to look for trogons. We told them, of course, about our success in finding them the day before and invited them to join us. Now we were five. Ten minutes out of the parking lot, a trogon glided over my right shoulder and landed in a tree about forty feet up the trail to give Tom and John their first look at this elusive wonder.

As we continued up the trail, we ran into Pat and Betty headed in the opposite direction. Pat had his binoculars with him this time. They had found the nest but hadn't seen any birds yet, so they turned around and joined us. Then we were seven. When we got there, the nest was right where it was supposed to be. Except for Steve and John, who went up the trail another twenty minutes or so, we all settled down to wait and see what would happen. We sat and talked and got acquainted. When John and Steve returned, we gave up on our vigil and started back down the trail, occasionally stopping to check out other birds.

Just as we got into the picnic area by the parking lot, we spotted a couple more trogons! Pat got all excited and ran off to get his larger binoculars for a better look. Several other people in the area—a lady in a wheelchair, her sister, and maybe a daughter of one or the other—joined us. They had been hoping to see a trogon. About to give up, instead they got sucked into our group. Then we were ten. Everyone was passing binoculars back and forth, trying to show everyone else the best views of the birds as they moved around in the trees. Pat, the manly game hunter, was just as excited as the rest of us.

By this time Ken, Irene, and Tyler were back. Now we were thirteen. Everyone got a good look at the trogons. As the party broke up, Tom and John shook hands with most of us a couple times and thanked us—for what I'm not sure they even knew, but everyone seemed pleased to have been part of the group for a little while. They were all really nice people—which is not at all unusual with birders. John gave Steve his address and suggested we come to New Orleans sometime to bird in the swamps with him.

The remaining six of us climbed back into the van and headed for Cave Creek Ranch. "Did you get checked in?" we asked. We got some mumbling from the three check-in specialists about how we needed to look at the place. This sounded ominous. We pulled in and drove back to a cabin they told us was the best of the lot. We eased our way into the unit, expecting the worst. We were not disappointed. It was a toilet. There had been no upkeep for years, and it looked like cleaning had ceased sometime before that. The shower had some sort of scientific experiment underway that looked downright scary. We all stood there speechless.

Then Ken revealed that the Portal Peak Inn (where we had been staying) had three rooms open that night due to cancellations. They had gone ahead and checked us in. The whole charade was apparently designed to make us feel thankful for having escaped this scummy rip-off of a place and grateful for the efforts of our three-member check-in committee. Relieved, we refrained from administering a significant emotional experience involving large sticks to the three miscreants.

[We have it on authority that the Cave Creek Ranch is since under new ownership and has been completely renovated.]

We had dinner at the store/restaurant again—where else? They had become completely accustomed to our strange behavior by this time and almost seemed to enjoy having us back. It's amazing what a good tip will do! The food, by the way, was great. Always an important issue for our gang.

So far on the trip, the weather had been clear and hot. The air was very dry, and we packed water on all hikes. The heat, dryness, and exertion just seemed to suck the moisture right out of us. I like the way people from Arizona try to sell their high temperatures and low humidity by explaining that it is a "dry heat." There are skeletons walking around the state muttering as they pass, "But it's a dry heat."

The next morning was our last full day of birding. We packed up and left Portal by six a.m., stopping at South Fork again to make one more try for the Strickland's Woodpecker. By this time Steve was convinced this particular woodpecker was avoiding him at all costs. He was taking it personally!

We drove up and out of the canyon just like the day before, but instead of turning off to Rustler Park, we crossed over the pass and took Pinery Canyon Road northwest to the Chiricahua National Monument. The Monument, about twelve-thousand square acres, contains large areas of volcanic rock which has eroded into pinnacles called "hoodoos." We saw hundreds of pinnacles that had large pieces of rock balanced on top, making them appear very top-heavy. They seemed to defy gravity. It would be a nice place to spend a day or so hiking if you weren't too particular about what might drop on your head. We drove the eight miles of paved loop road through the monument marveling at the strange scenery and, of course, looking for birds.

The Sewage Ponds of Willcox—A Birder's Paradise?

Our next destination—I know this will excite you all—was the sewage ponds at Willcox, a small town on Interstate 10 between the Chiricahua National Monument and Tucson. Do we know how to live or what? We actually found some small lakes, home to birds, behind

the ponds. Several of the birds were new ones for this trip, so it was a surprisingly productive stop. Sewage ponds from any sizable town or city can be quite productive for finding birds, but it requires getting used to the attack on the olfactory senses. Most birdwatchers go, but they don't talk about it all that much. Especially when socializing with a group of casual acquaintances during, say, an opera intermission.

Back to Tucson—Journey's End

We had promised Tyler that we would get into Tucson early enough to play some tennis and go swimming. As soon as we checked into our hotel, we grabbed our rackets and headed for a tennis club in town. It was five in the afternoon, and the temperature hovered right around 101 degrees. This is actually cool for Tucson, as evidenced by locals wearing jackets. On the cement courts I'm not sure how hot it was. Definitely hotter than 101.

Tyler was the only one among us who had recently played tennis. For the rest of us, it had been years. By the time we warmed up (really sick pun) and played a set, we were ready to bag it. Although she didn't have a racket, Lorraine came with us to rest and watch. But we kept her on the go chasing balls that had gone into the next courts or over the fences. She got a good workout without swinging a racket.

We had dinner at the Good Earth restaurant and then sat round the pool watching Ken and Tyler swim.

The next morning after Ken took Steve and Tyler to their plane, the remaining four of us had breakfast, checked out of our hotel, and headed for the Arizona-Sonora Desert Museum. What an amazing place! It was hotter than Hades but very interesting. We took a tour and learned all about the plants and animals of the Sonoran Desert. The most interesting thing was the description of what Arizona looked like 150 years ago. With the ground water only about four feet below the surface, most of the now-barren valleys were grass-covered riparian areas with marshes and lots of cottonwood trees. It must have been much like the environment we had explored at the Nature Conservancy preserve back in Patagonia.

By the time we finished our tour at the Arizona-Sonora Desert Museum, it was time to head for the airport.

It had been a great six days, leaving us champing at the bit for more.

Here's a list of birds we saw on this trip, roughly in the order of sighting:

Scott's Oriole, Black-headed Grosbeak, Painted Redstart, Phainopepla, House Wren, White-breasted Nuthatch, Bridled Titmouse, Gray-breasted Jay, Acorn Woodpecker, Blue-throated Hummingbird, Broad-billed Hummingbird, Summer Tanager, Hepatic Tanager, Sulphur-bellied Flycatcher, Anna's Hummingbird, Magnificent Hummingbird, Bronzed Cowbird, Bewick's Wren, Broad-tailed Hummingbird, White-eared Hummingbird, Elf Owl, Northern Oriole, Brown Towhee, Golden-crowned Kinglet, Canyon Wren, Pygmy Nuthatch, Red-breasted Nuthatch, Mexican Chickadee, Western Flycatcher, Greater Pewee, White-throated Swift, Elegant Trogon, Scaled Quail, White-crowned Sparrow, Eastern Phoebe, Rufous-sided Towhee, Common Yellowthroat, Northern Cardinal, Yellow Warbler, Gray Vireo, Blue Grosbeak, Yellow-breasted Chat, Rose-throated Becard, Black Phoebe, Gila Woodpecker, Violet-crowned Hummingbird, Turkey Vulture, Black-throated Gray Warbler, Loggerhead Shrike, Hermit Thrush, Western Bluebird, Brown Creeper, Common Raven, Piñon Jay, Vermilion Flycatcher, Cassin's Kingbird, White-winged Dove, and Green Kingfisher.

Chapter Two

A Taste of the Gulf

On a bright spring morning Lorraine and I left our fair part of Texas (Fort Worth) and drove south to Houston, where we had hotel reservations. We ate an excellent dinner—or at least we think we did. Everything tasted like recycled cardboard because both of us were on antibiotics for the "Texas Crud" which was making the rounds of nearly everybody we knew—and me for the second time. It's nice to be wanted, but I could have done without the rerun. This Texas Crud wasn't life-threatening, mind you, but it brought with it a complete lack of appetite (well, that's life-threatening for me), a queasy stomach, a very sore throat, a congested chest, double vision, and a serious loss of short term memory.

Because of that last item, none of my co-workers even noticed I was also under the weather.

[Now there's a term I've never understood: "under the weather." Have you ever heard of anyone being "over the weather"? Furthermore, considering how gravity holds us to the surface of the planet, aren't we all beneath the weather? If given some time I bet I could conjure up—er, I mean *discover*—where that phraseology originated. But I digress, and it's probably not the last time.]

Assembling Our Team

The next morning, after visiting several warehouse/showrooms looking for an alternate site to our current Houston operation, we checked out of the hotel and headed to Houston's Hobby Airport to meet Steve and Tyler, who were flying in from Kentucky, and Ken and Irene from Washington. You've met these four people before.

Before meeting the first arrivals, we picked up the twelve-passenger van waiting for us at National Car Rental. We wondered whether Steve and Tyler would actually make it on the announced flight, as they have a history of only intermittent success at catching planes, primarily due to Steve's bodily functions and his propensity to daydream when enclosed in confined areas. To our relief they arrived on time, looking fit and ready for action. The only glitch? Tyler's checked luggage failed to arrive with him.

We took Steve and Tyler out to the van and went back with our Town Car and the van to meet Ken and Irene.

Let me say a word about the van. This was a Dodge Maxi-Ram. It stands about ten feet tall, and seats twelve people, with two bucket seats up front and three bench seats and a luggage area stretching off to the "back forty." It's about as comfortable for eight passengers as it's possible to be. Of course that's easy for *me* to say. I spent most of my van time in the driver's seat.

The only downside to these vans for birders is that all the windows behind the driver are tinted. There was a tendency to describe every flying and creeping thing as being darker than it actually was. This color confusion was soon overcome by most of our party as they learned to color-correct on the fly, so to speak. Even my brother-in-law Ted got over his "black bird" phase after a day or two. More about that later.

Ken and Irene came in on time and they looked great. Lorraine and Irene took our Town Car, while the rest of us piled into the van. We hopped onto Interstate 10 and headed east to Winnie, Texas—a small town about twenty miles directly north of High Island—more or less the focal point of this year's outing.

I might as well expand on this geography thing while I still have your attention.

High Island, elevation 38 feet, is about a half-mile inland from the Gulf of Mexico. The town sits on a tall (well, in southeast Texas it's tall) salt dome, making it one of the highest points on the Gulf Coast and giving it an "island" effect. This particular time of year birds congregate on the Yucatan Peninsula in Mexico. Then, for some reason known only to them, they take off in great flocks and fly all night across six hundred miles of Gulf water to the Texas coast. If the winds are with them, they make it all the way across the Gulf and continue inland. But if the winds are just a little adverse, the exhausted birds land on the first thing they come to on the Texas Coast, which is usually High Island, home to a number of bird sanctuaries. Birders can see species here that they would not normally encounter otherwise. During spring migrations it is reputed to be one of the top birding places in the U.S. Once the birds have rested, they take to the air and continue north, some flying as far as northern Canada.

Fallout!

Experienced birders tell of great clouds of birds composed of numerous species flying overhead or settling down on nearby trees and shrubbery, so tired they can hardly move. Birders are able to inspect them at very close range. And photography? Oh my! It's been reported by photographers that tired birds can be adjusted, moved to better light, and virtually posed with their full cooperation. It sounded like our kind of place.

When birds arrive in great gobs like this, it's called a "fallout." This part of the Gulf held a lot of promise for us intrepid adventurers.

Getting Settled in Winnie

When we arrived in Winnie, Ted and Dorothy were already checked in but not on the premises. We unloaded, hung around for a respectable time waiting for them to return—at least two minutes—and then left to get some food. As we exited the motel parking lot, we passed a vehicle with a passenger I thought I recognized, so we turned around and followed it back to the motel. Sure enough, it was Ted and Dorothy.

This was the first time they had joined us on one of these expeditions. We were delighted to have them along—me especially, as it gave me someone who knew less about birds than I did. Sad to say, that edge only lasted for about two days.

After a flurry of greetings, we climbed into the van and went off in search of dinner. Now Winnie is a small town (about 2,300 population) on a major cross-country freeway. Good eating places appear to be against the law. The most promising place we found was an establishment called Al-T's Seafood and Steakhouse—a southeast Texas/Louisiana sort of place. The menu, which appeared to offer a real taste of the

Gulf, explained that they could serve up shrimp forty different ways, along with several dishes involving "gator." Yes, boys and girls, that's alligator. Looking back later, after seeing them in their natural habitat I'm still not entirely clear which part or parts they were serving.

Included with all this were the area's favorites: "dirty rice" (don't even ask), and "boudin." As explained to me by one waitress, boudin is a Cajun Creole Louisiana sausage that contains everything people in these parts won't knowingly eat face-to-face. Although we weren't in Louisiana, we were evidently close enough. I've never found a boudin-maker who would look me straight in the eye and explain, without blushing, what he put in the stuff. They don't waste a thing.

In spite of the exotic menu, we all managed to get plenty of good food to eat.

In the fading twilight after dinner, we drove down to High Island and wandered around one of the bird sanctuaries there. It was so dark we couldn't see a thing. We finally returned to our motel, filled with anticipation for the day to come.

The rest of the evening, we sat around talking and negotiating a start time for the next morning. I'd better explain this. On past trips we would decide, after being subjected by some of our party to the old adage about the early bird getting the worm, that we needed to start no later than 5:00 a.m. Ken, unable to sleep, would come knocking at our doors around 4:30 a.m., enticing us with some far-fetched story about having heard the mating call of the Twill-beaked Cornhusker. By that time, since we were awake anyway and the Cornhusker was high on our list, we figured we might as well head out. Steve was only a couple steps behind Ken in this treacherous behavior, evidently having inherited the defective gene.

This night, to everyone's amazement, we all agreed on an 8:00 a.m. start time.

I should enlighten the reader here on Ted's lifestyle. Ted enjoys the late evening and early morning hours as a time to reflect on life and generally get anything done that needs doing. Getting up is not a high priority for Ted, especially when he's on vacation. When he and Dorothy got sucked into—I mean *agreed*—to join us on this quest, one of their stipulations was that Ted could sleep in and join us at some point during the day when his physiology told him it was appropriate. We all cheered the next morning when Ted was on deck at 8:00 a.m. raring to go.

The motel offered a small breakfast buffet in the office where we could choose from an assortment of rolls, coffee, and juice. We cleaned the place out and hightailed it south.

On to High Island

The road from Winnie to High Island travels through farmland, past some decent wetlands—ponds and roadside ditches filled with water—and over a bridge crossing the Gulf Intracoastal Waterway. This country along the Gulf is very flat, so a little water goes a long way. In other words, some great bird habitat. On this, our first day out, we stopped for everything—English sparrows, blackbirds, grackles, egrets, herons, bitterns, ibis, and anything else that flew, waded, or even twitched. Every morning we traveled this road, we saw a wide variety of birds.

Let me explain a little about how our group works. There were eight of us in the van, all looking out the windows for birds or anything else that might grab our fancy. At any moment anyone could (and would) shout out for the driver to stop the van, back it up, move it forward slightly while please not sinking into the roadside marsh or getting hit from behind by an eighteen-wheel refinery tanker full of high-octane death.

During this part of the trip, we drove on two-lane roads with speed limits of 70 mph (remember, we're in Texas).

Luckily for us, this part of the state is somewhat tolerant of birders and their strange highway antics. It didn't help much that this group had recently learned that the driver (that's me) was currently serving a sentence of two nights in traffic school having recently run afoul of law enforcement in this very area. Every time we had a near-death experience on the roads, this subject surfaced and was bandied about until the driver (me) was again suitably humbled and fully safety conscious.

So we would drive, stop, look, identify, and drive on. As this was Dorothy and Ted's maiden birding voyage, we didn't expect them to meet the high level of expertise to which the rest of us had become accustomed. But we did begin to wonder about Ted when, by the end of the first day, he was still shouting, "Oh look, there's another one of those black birds!" He eventually got over this phase, and both he and Dorothy became a credit to the sport before the trip was over. It took us two hours of this "stop, look, identify, and drive on" to reach High Island that first morning.

Early in the day, Steve felt compelled to recount to Dorothy and Ted my history of running over birds with a van. He just wouldn't let it rest. He made it sound as if the list of birds dead at my hands was without end. All that just because I accidentally ran over an Acorn Woodpecker in Arizona's Madera Canyon on a previous trip. Steve makes me sound like some kind of maniacal bird killer, which of course I'm not—at least the bird killer part. It was only that one time, and I did demonstrate some remorse. As of this writing, not one wildlife area in this country or any neighboring sovereign state has my wanted poster on a public information bulletin board. If they can forget, why not my own family? I'm just asking.

High Island is a tiny town where we visited two bird sanctuaries established by the Audubon Society—Boy Scout Woods and Smith Oaks. The reason for the sanctuaries at

High Island was explained earlier, and if you've forgotten, you'll just have to backtrack and look it up. If I have to keep repeating myself we'll never get this over with, and we don't want that now, do we?

Our first prolonged stop was at Boy Scout Woods. We bought our Audubon patches, which gave us the right to wander around in these woods, getting bit by mosquitoes and spraining our necks. Audubon patches are the Society's way of getting revenue to support birding habitats. It's a very reasonable price to pay for such wonderful entertainment.

The Family Birding Curse

Now I must explain something embarrassing about my family birding group. Just by showing up, we seem to instantly turn a hot birding area into a mediocre one. We've not yet figured out the mechanism, but finding a solution to this phenomenon is high on our list of priorities, right after eating, sleeping, and having fun. We know this ability we possess isn't restricted by geography, as we've seen it everywhere we've gone.

For the first couple of years we just shrugged it off and paraphrased Yogi Berra: "If the birds don't wanna come out, nobody's gonna stop them."

To illustrate, we immediately found out that only days before our arrival here at High Island, there had been a fallout of stupendous proportions. Visitors saw nearly every species known to man. But today, as the Audubon people explained, the only bird seen so far was one Blue Jay who stole part of their breakfast. They assured us that another fallout could happen at any moment. Hope springs eternal....

We wandered around the woods searching for any movement or color that might signal a bird. Spotting the bird, of course, is only the first part of the endeavor. To any serious birder, identifying what you've seen is the thing. There are two reasons for this. One, so you can put it on your bird list, or "life list" as it's called by some because really serious birders usually don't have a life outside of birding. Two, so you can tell the next birder you meet what you just saw. This must be done with style, grace, and just the right amount of authority—which, strange as it may seem, has a lot to do with the clothes you are wearing, the amount of facial hair you have, and your accent. We'll meet an example later.

The Identification Conundrum

Let's talk a little more about this identifying thing. Some birds are of a size, or have such singularity of markings, that even I can get one right now and again. This category includes hawks and eagles as a group, ostriches, turkeys, and a few other species.

One of the peculiarities of migration is that about forty-seven species of warblers and another thirty-two species of vireos, give or take, may pass through High Island at one time. The difference between any of these warblers and/or vireos may be two feathers which are dark blue rather than black, or maybe light gray instead of white, or maybe four and one-half wing bars versus five. The colors and markings can change with the seasons, the sex, and/or the age of the bird. So you have mating plumage, spring plumage, molting plumage, and winter plumage. Then there is the juvenile first-year plumage, juvenile second-year plumage, and juvenile going-through-a-rebellious-stage plumage. These birds are all about the size of your average leaf.

So here we were, walking around on the forest floor, gazing up into the forest canopy—all fluttering leaves and twigs—looking for birds that are masters of camouflage and obviously on some kind of stimulants (all talk of tired birds falling out of the sky notwithstanding), evidenced by the way they jump about while we're trying our best to identify them. When we do spot one, likely as not, it's directly between us and the sun, rendering all attempts at identification futile. If these birds have any sense of humor at all, they should be full of enough endorphins after playing with us to fly nonstop to Hudson's Bay and still be giggling when they get there. All I'm trying to say is that identifying birds can be time-consuming and dicey. For me it's the least exciting part of our excursions.

We walked around Boy Scout Woods for a couple of hours, seeing a few birds but nothing new or special. Two things motivated us to leave: the lack of birds and hunger—not necessarily in that order.

Galveston, O Galveston

From High Island we drove south to the coast, only about a half-mile away, and then turned southwest toward Galveston. Across the channel from Galveston lies a point of land known as Bolivar Peninsula, home to Bolivar Flats Shorebird Sanctuary, our next destination.

To get there we had to drive over Rollover Fish Pass, which is nothing more than a narrow channel through which the Gulf pours into east Galveston Bay during incoming tides, evidently bringing with it lots of good things to eat. On the bay side, not too far from shore, we found all kinds of water birds.

Shortly after Rollover Pass, we spied a sign promoting an "over-the-water" restaurant. We followed the road out onto a peninsula, and sure enough, we found a place to eat. As with past dubious enterprises, Steve and I were commissioned to investigate and make sure the place was up to our standards. Of course the hungrier the group is, the lower the standards become. Mostly it is a way for the rest of the group to finger someone else if the place turns out to be less than what they wanted, whatever that was. It would go like this, "Why did you drag us into this stinky, dirty, slow-service, loud-music, full-of-rednecks, nothing-I-can-eat place?"

In any event, Steve and I gave a thumbs-up to this one. We entered, ordered, and waited. The water mentioned in their advertising was the Intracoastal Waterway, so we had a great view of passing barges and smaller watercraft. The combination of the smells from the canal, close-by wetlands, diesel fumes from passing boats, and dead marine life along the canal, helped create an ambiance that would be hard to match. We waited for our food; and then we waited for our food some more. It had to have been the slowest service in the Western Hemisphere, but the food finally arrived and we gobbled it down.

I should explain at this point that we really did feel sorry for people who had to serve us in any way. As you know, we're all related. And we all laugh easily. As a family we have numerous insider things that, combined with current events, will send us into gales of laughter. For those around us who don't understand what sets us off, it may seem that we are laughing at them or trying to make them feel uncomfortable. But nothing could be further from the truth. During these times together we just laugh a lot. One trip with the family is better than a whole year's worth of prescription drugs.

Bolivar Flats

At Bolivar Flats you can drive out onto and along the Gulf beach for quite a ways and then walk into the protected area. While driving along the beach we saw numerous gulls, terns, and sandpipers.

The only things harder to identify than—well, several species—are sandpipers. Still in the van at this point, we could drive pretty close to these birds, but we still had no idea which sandpipers we were looking at.

Dorothy and Ted then got their first taste of what we call "democratic bird-identification." This decision-making process is based on what each individual thinks it is, how bad each individual wants to move along, and which birds we still don't have on our list. Taking all this into consideration, each member of the party gives an opinion on a possible identification, and the majority opinion usually rules.

The Natives Are Restless

By the time we were finished with Bolivar Flats I began to sense the vibrations of our first mutiny.

The group had agreed to bird in southeast Texas knowing full well that amenities (such as they probably weren't even used to), would be few and far between. Everyone knew this going in and had agreed to this Spartan existence beforehand. Now I picked up on—and mind you this was only the late afternoon of our first full day of birding—a furtive plan to force the driver to take them to the bright lights and fleshpots of Galveston. If this group had been with Moses and the Children of Israel, they never would have made it to the Promised Land! I'm not one to name names, but I'm sure Irene was the one who subtly got this idea going. As we used to say in Latin, "Dux femina facti." (A woman was leader of the exploit.) I put up a stout resistance until Ted agreed to buy dinner for everyone.

The rebels had won.

We took the ferry across the channel to Galveston. These ferries are small, but there are a half-dozen plying the bay all the time, so there was no wait. We boarded right away, and the boat headed out into the bay. A slew of seagulls flapped around the stern of the boat waiting for a handout. The only thing we had on board the van that we were willing to give to seagulls was a bag of gummy worms. A gummy worm is second cousin to a gummy bear, but instead of being cute and squiggly, it is repulsive and squiggly. But it tastes the same.

Someone had purchased five pounds of this edible plastic to stave off insurrections associated with hunger. You can see how effective that idea turned out to be.

Back to the seagulls—I would grasp a gummy worm in my fingers and hold my hand out the window above the roofline and wait. The gulls would swoop down and snatch the worm out of my fingers. With my anticipatory shakiness and the gulls' possible bad eyesight, they had a hard time distinguishing between gummy worms and my fingers. Since I couldn't see them coming, it was rather a shock when one of them suddenly struck. We never actually saw a gull eat a gummy worm, but we did see a couple of them haul the squiggly things around for a while, then unobtrusively drop them into the drink. Nutritionally speaking, a gull is not as dumb as one might think.

When the ferry docked in Galveston, we drove around town until everyone was well-saturated with that big city buzz. But that wasn't enough. The group also demanded a place to eat. With no idea where to find one, I just continued driving around until we finally stumbled onto an Italian restaurant which turned out to be excellent. I tried to convince everyone I knew where I was going the whole time, but no one bought it. Their show of amazement that I found anything at all *could* have been somewhat more restrained. In any event, it was a happy bunch of campers that got back in the van and headed toward Winnie.

Tennis Anyone?

One of the evolving traditions of our birding expeditions is that we play some tennis at least once during our sojourn. The first time we did this was in Tucson on a day when it seemed to be about one hundred and twenty-five degrees in the shade. That the elders in our group survived at all was a miracle.

Anyway, here we were at 9:00 p.m. in Winnie when Tyler proposed that we go and play tennis on some very nice lighted courts at the local school. When I took the cover off my racket I discovered that I had broken a string back in Tucson and had never gotten it fixed. Knowing my racket would play like a flat zucchini, I demanded a handicap of some sort, but no one paid me any mind.

Steve and Tyler took the end of the court where they didn't have to look into the lights, and Ken and I—ever the compassionate sportsmen—took what was left. We volleyed for a while and then played a set, which Ken and I won in spite of some new-age score-keeping by Tyler. By this time Steve was holding his chest and I was limping from a pulled something in the back of one leg, so we left the court to the others to play a few more games. Ken would be there yet, if we hadn't hauled him off with us.

Ted had stayed in his motel room to read. It was a story about a birder who was bright enough to be a detective. Obviously fiction.

The next morning we left at 8:00 a.m. after raiding the office breakfast bar again. They were watching for us, but we descended on them before they could hide the food. Ted filled his thermos, and Irene carried away enough pastry to fill the whole group, even though we were all in there getting our own. I never did know what she did with all of it.

We quickly realized that the motel people had our number as far as free breakfasts were concerned. The next morning we would need to come up with some other tactic for filling up.

Back to High Island

We headed once again for High Island, hoping for one of those "fallout" days. This time we stopped first at the Audubon Society's Smith Oaks Bird Sanctuary a for a while. We saw a number of birds in a big tree that was mostly covered with lavender wisteria. Quite a sight. We found a few birds, including a bittern sitting in a tree, but definitely no fallout.

Steve had decided that the main focus of this trip should be to spot a Painted Bunting. When we arrived at Smith Oaks we were informed that just minutes before we got there six Painted Buntings had left the small dead tree in the parking lot. Steve's decision that some bird or another was a must-see on any trip was the kiss of death. We never would catch sight of that particular bird. Everyone else in a three-state area would have seen this bird just yesterday or this morning, but not us. Now it looked like the Painted Bunting was going to be another such triumph.

As I strolled through Smith Oak Woods, I spotted a large turtle about fourteen inches from snout to tail. Of course I had to pick it up. It was the only thing in the woods moving slower than me. As I held the turtle in my hand, it took a whiz. Luckily I was pointing his back end away from me at the time. Otherwise, given the highly developed olfactory senses of the other passengers, the rest of the day could have been a little strained. For such a small critter, that turtle sure held a lot of liquid.

After we'd beaten the bushes, so to speak, pretty thoroughly, we headed back to another Audubon Society bird sanctuary, popularly known as "Boy Scout Woods," about a half-mile away. We walked the trails and shook the trees, but didn't find much to crow about.

By this time we were all hungry, so we stopped at the small (and only) café in High Island. After lunch we drove down to the Gulf and took Highway 87 east along the beach.

After a couple miles, our timid group made the driver turn around—just because the road had quit. Well, it hadn't really quit, but the large "ROAD CLOSED" sign about a mile back had put them in a skittish mood. When we began to encounter large portions of the roadway that had been washed away by the surf, they vocally (shrilly, I might add) voted to turn around. We stopped at some ponds on the way back to the junction and found a lot of birds, including some Roseate Spoonbills.

Next, we cruised to Anahuac National Wildlife Refuge, several miles northwest of High Island. We drove around on the dike roads for an hour or two. In addition to the many birds, we saw numerous alligators. We watched a while as one of these big crocodilians stalked a Tricolored Heron. The group was pretty evenly split between cheering for the 'gator and cheering for the heron. At the last minute the heron wandered out of harm's way.

This area also boasted many rather large nutria. At another stop on our rounds of Anahuac, we watched a 'gator stalk one of these large rodents. This time the 'gator was the clear favorite, perhaps because it was late in the day and everyone was hungry again, empathizing with the 'gator.

After driving all the dike roads, we drove across the wildlife refuge toward the edge of the bay. The land was flat as a griddle, with little to offer a crew of intrepid birders.

However, along the road we spotted a snake. I backed up until it was just below the driver-side door. It turned out to be a Cottonmouth (or Water Moccasin to you rural readers) just lying motionless alongside the road. Its body was swollen in the middle, indicating it had recently eaten. I threw some gummy worms at it to see if it was alive. The Cottonmouth reared up, opening wide its very white mouth. Naturally I had to snap pictures with every camera that came flying to the front of the van.

A little farther along, we came up behind two ladies in an auto, just poking along. I kept hoping the driver would pull over so I could pass. Finally she did, but just as I started to make my move she suddenly swung sharply to the left, neatly blocking the road. My first thought was, "Well, here it is at last." Steve had warned me that the Arizona Acorn Woodpecker family was going to put out a contract on me for killing one of their own. I expected to see these two ladies jump out of the car with guns spitting lead. But no, they were just trying to turn around.

I easily stopped in time to avoid a crash, and we were amused to realize that the driver had no idea we were even there, although my passing maneuver and subsequent abrupt stop left us very close to her. She backed up and finally got her car positioned so that she could swing around and go back the way she had come. That's when she looked out her side window and saw this big van sitting a couple of yards away. Her expression was worth the wait. I backed up some and she was able to come on around us. By that time she was as tickled with herself as we were with her. It's probably just as well she couldn't hear any of the derisive comments coming from the back of our van. As far as I was concerned, it was nice to sit back and let someone else take the heat about driving skills for a change.

As we neared town the old hue and cry arose: "Where are we going to eat?" (Do you notice an ongoing theme with this group?) As I've mentioned before, Winnie had limited opportunities. We drove through town looking at and critiquing the usual freeway-interchange eateries plus a couple of marginal-looking Mexican restaurants. The excuses for not stopping at any of these varied from too dirty, had a bad experience with a similar one three states away, didn't like the looks of the place, had too many customers, or didn't have enough customers.

We finally settled on Pizza Inn as the least scary of the lot. They pushed together a bunch of tables and got us settled, but before we could order, the group made me go back into the kitchen and bring out three pizza pans so they could assess the three sizes of pizza available on the menu. Just as I took my seat after that greasy project, the waitress came and started to refill my and Lorraine's root-beer glasses. Lorraine had pushed her glass toward me so the waitress could reach it better. When the glass was full, Lorraine, looking at Irene, started to slide it back toward herself when it caught the edge of the abutting table. The full glass started to tip toward her. Not wanting to be drenched in root beer, Lorraine gave her glass a whack to straighten it up.

Said whack would have sent her glass into the next county if it hadn't hit *my* glass and sent them both toward Ken, myself, and the waitress. We all leaped back and managed to escape the brown frothy deluge. The waitress got us a roll of paper towels. When the mess was cleaned up, she looked us over thoughtfully and walked away, leaving the towels with us. Smart girl.

Lorraine Steps Up

During this whole trip, by the way, Lorraine had once again fallen into the role of Tribe Scribe, which meant keeping a written record of all the sightings—at least the verified ones. People would shout out that they saw something, and Lorraine was supposed to get it into the book. But then a little later someone else would counter that what we saw back there must be something else and not what the identifier first thought. Nobody ever knew which particular bird that something back there had been in the first place, so Lorraine had to try to sort all this out. She did a splendid job. Along with Ken, she was one of the two really patient and serious identifiers. The lists at the end of each chapter and in the appendix are hers.

High Island Again

The following morning we were out and on our way to High Island at 8:00 a.m., still hoping for a fallout. We made a quick stop at Smith Oaks again to check the Painted Bunting tree, but it was bare. I'm absolutely convinced that immediately upon our departure, seventeen Painted Buntings lit in the tree and stayed until just before we came back the next morning.

Next we went back to Boy Scout Woods. Since it was now the weekend, the place was crawling with birders. Close to the front gate, someone had set up two small grandstands to accommodate as many watchers as possible. This seating overlooked a small clearing with a little pond in it.

At this pond we found at least forty-five people all staring at an Indigo Bunting, which is, oddly enough, a small, indigo-colored bunting. If looks could kill, this poor bird would either be in birdie heaven or birdie hell. (Of course, as someone commented, whether this particular bunting would have chosen heaven for the climate or hell for the company, we had no way of knowing.) In the Woods that day we practically had to take a number before looking. There were at least fifteen people for every visible bird.

Farther on into the woods we came to what some enthusiastic nature-lover has dubbed "the Cathedral." It is an approximately one thousand square-foot clearing with a boardwalked floor and benches around the edges, sitting smack dab in the middle of a grove of tall trees. Under the trees thick bushes obscure any decent views close to the ground. We joined a group of about seventy people, all hoping to see something wonderful.

When someone spotted a smallish, leaf-colored bird in the overhead canopy of small leaves, seventy pairs of binoculars were simultaneously trained in that direction, sixty-five of the birders asking, "Where is it?" and four of the five remaining people asking, "What is it?" The one remaining guy gave it a glance and remarked casually, "That's a second-season, juvenile, male, 'Semiplumulated Vireo,' but with the 'northern-Mexican-variant' tail markings."

Now because this guy had a beard, spoke with a British accent, and was wearing a bush jacket and beat up jungle hat, nobody questioned his guess. Instead, you could hear responses like, "Oh yeah, I can see that now," or Steve's, "Sure enough, I was just about to say that." (Nobody had any idea that this guy was a guest of the "Texas Institution for the Care and Feeding of Actors with Mad Cow Disease" and that for therapy, he had been sent out on weekends to make like a birding expert—well, at least this is what passed through my mind as he offered his wisdom.) Keep in mind that as birdwatchers we are among a select group of oft-confused people. Any voice of authority is a port in a storm.

In the midst of all this activity, someone spotted a Swainson's Warbler creeping about in the nearby bushes. Suddenly, as if controlled by a puppeteer, everyone moved over to spot the little fellow (the bird, that is). Of course we, needing one of these warblers for our list, were there right along with the rest of them.

Please understand that this bird is small, and to put it as positively as possible, mottled with thirteen shades of brown. It was flitting around on the brown ground, on the dead brown limbs, and in the low, mostly brown bushes, holding still for at most a tenth of a second at a time. Dorothy could not spot the thing for the life of her, which is not a comment on her aging eyesight. Finally, one of the "experts" grabbed her by the back of the neck and pushed her face into the bushes far enough for her to get a glimpse. (Gotta love these birders!)

As the little bird moved from spot to spot, the whole group would move right along with it as if they were one, somewhat disjointed, body. It was quite something to watch the watchers, which I fell back to do as soon as I finally spotted the suspect warbler myself.

Once again we left Boy Scout Woods and High Island without experiencing a fallout or seeing our Painted Bunting.

Sabine

We headed next for Sabine National Wildlife Refuge. To get there we had to drive back up to Winnie, across to Port Arthur, down to the Gulf coast, east along the coast into Louisiana, and then north to the refuge. Between Port Arthur and the coast, we stopped at a little convenience store advertising sandwiches and picked up some sustenance.

Once again, this whole area is extremely flat, only about six inches above a good high tide. The flatness seemed to make Steve a little nervous. Without his Kentucky hills and hollers he must have felt exposed and insecure.

We walked the trails at Sabine, most of which are boardwalks over and through a large marshy area. As Dorothy pointed out to us, this really *was* a marsh; a swamp would be the same thing in the woods. Or vice-versa. I can't quite remember now.

We saw a number of 'gators and got close up and personal with several ibis. These birds are very glossy and rather neat-looking. But whether we were seeing Glossy Ibis or White-faced Ibis, I had no idea. To tell the difference I would have to hold one of each by the neck under a magnifying glass. Luckily for me, there were others in our group who were confident they could tell the difference.

Leaving the wildlife refuge, we drove back to Port Arthur and took Highway 87 down to the coast. This highway goes right through the middle of an oil refinery, a blight on the landscape and offensive to the eye and nose. But I keep buying gas and am thankful for it, just like everyone else.

We made a stop at the Sabine Pass Battleground State Historic Site in order to educate the foreigners (read "Yankees") in the group about the part that a few heroic Texans had played in defending this area during the "Dastardly War against the South," as it's referred to in these parts.

After soaking up all the history we could at the historic site, we continued down to Texas Point National Wildlife Refuge—a wildlife area that covers the southeasternmost point of land in Texas. To do this area justice one really needs a boat, which we didn't have—our boat-sized van notwithstanding.

For the next place on our list we had to delve into Ken's book, "*Every Southeastern Texas Birding Place You Ever Wanted to Hear About, Plus.*" It told us about a place called "Sabine Woods," giving directions and mileage and ending by telling us that the entrance was a metal gate we could open if we wanted to enter. We checked the mileage, followed the directions, and found the metal gate, which was nearly overgrown with—well, growing stuff. Problem was, this gate clearly hadn't been opened for many years. We quickly abandoned any hope of getting in.

Sea Rim State Park

By this time it was getting late in the afternoon and certain members of the group were getting rebellious again, having the notion they should be fed. Still following Ken's book, we were looking for a certain boat dock that had attracted some Cave Swallows. But the book's directions didn't make sense to us. Ignoring the book, we left the park, drove down the road, and turned into McFadden National Wildlife Area. We got as far as a closed gate (again).

The hunger rebellion kept building momentum until we found them some Yellow-crowned Night-Herons to observe. Also, tossing some gummy worms in their direction seemed to distract them—the birding party that is, not the herons.

We made one more stop at Sea Rim State Park, where the more ambitious of us hiked the boardwalk through the wetlands. But we saw nothing new. On the way back to Port Arthur we did find the missing boat dock. But no Cave Swallows. However, Ken did manage to scare a young 'gator near to death. Which reminds me of a story my imaginary late Great-Uncle Velanoff Spady wrote in his journal. (Digression warning!) Velanoff, after emigrating from Russia one jump ahead of the...well, that's not part of this story—traveled extensively as a member of a vaudeville troupe. The story from Velanoff's journal goes like this:

On my first trip to Florida I had occasion to watch a woman wrestle a large lizard the locals called an alligator. I will not say she was big, but I do believe she had the reptile at a weight disadvantage. They blindfolded her and lowered her into a pit. I guess they were afraid she would not go into that pit if she could see what was down there. Anyway, after fighting that alligator for about one hour, she came up with a very nice, if somewhat large, alligator handbag, which was probably very useful to her as it gave her an easy way to carry her foot.

(I never actually had the pleasure of meeting great-uncle Velanoff, but I'm sure he was not one to exaggerate, let alone prevaricate.)

At Port Arthur we stopped and had a very good Mexican meal, which momentarily put a lid on the rebellion. Then we drove into the sunset all the way back to Winnie.

We spent the evening sitting around talking and looking at pictures of Lorraine's recent trip to Romania.

Only the Brave

I know there are those of you who think that birding is for feeble people who can't handle a real outdoor activity like hunting, fishing, snipe-snatching, or rodeo clowning. But let me tell you that birding is not for the faint of heart. It takes an intrepid watcher to hike the trails and beat the brush the way our group did on this trip. In one of the areas we visited, our group passed the following sign with only a slight shudder and a barely perceptible slowing of pace. The sign read:

BEWARE
Hazards Exist in this Sanctuary. There are:
Fire Ants
Poison Ivy
Alligators
Poisonous Snakes
Slippery Boardwalks
Armadillo Holes in the Trails
Etc.

Now wouldn't that give you pause? I've talked to hunters who have stood stock-still facing a wounded, charging Cape Buffalo without so much as batting an eye. But did they have to worry about armadillo holes, slippery boardwalks, or even turtles with bladder problems? I think not. So the next time you feel the urge to sneer at a birder, just remember we have been in, usually voluntarily, some equally dicey spots.

Homeward Bound

The next day most of us would have to leave for home, except for Ken and Irene who wanted to spend a few days exploring Houston. Because Steve and Tyler's plane was not leaving until 1:30, we would have a little time to—wait for it—**LOOK FOR BIRDS!** But next morning, just a little before 8:00 a.m., Steve came banging on our door in a panic with the news that the flight time was not 1:30, but actually 10:30!

It was about a ninety minute drive to the airport and he was rapidly developing a case of the fantods, more than mildly frantic to get going. We gave Steve the keys to the van and sent him and Tyler on their way.

Despite a falling mist, the rest of us piled into our Town Car and drove down to High Island again. We did Boy Scout Woods and saw very little. Then we went to Smith Oaks and saw even less. Before giving up, we tried the other side of Smith Oaks (actually the front entrance), and saw a handful of birds. By this time it had stopped misting and moved on to rain, so we packed it in and took off for the motel.

Ken, Irene, Lorraine, and I packed the Town Car, bid farewell to Dorothy and Ted, and headed for Houston Hobby Airport. We dropped Ken and Irene at the Hobby Hilton, and Lorraine and I drove home.

In Conclusion

As you can imagine, on a trip like this more gets done than just birding. Not having seen Dorothy and Ted for some time, it was great catching up with them again. It had also been quite a while since we had seen Ken, Irene, Steve, and Tyler. Just hanging out with them all was nice. I also picked up some useful tips on screwdriver usage that I won't go into here, and a secret formula for discouraging moles and maybe even Texas gophers. (Remember that Ken, Dorothy, and Steve are all medical professionals.) The formula must be kept secret, because if it works in Texas, Ken and I are going to make a fortune on this. Besides, if it doesn't work out, it would be much too embarrassing to have told anyone.

We just may have hooked Ted and Dorothy on this birding thing. By the time it was over, they spotted as well as anyone. As for identifying—well, it was amusing anyway.

Lorraine's list is at the end of the chapter, and I'm sure Ted's "Red-winged Cardinal" and "Shimmering Ibis" are on there with the rest of our sightings.

We think we have a place picked out for next year, but we want to make all the reservations, probably under assumed names, before we alert anyone as to where we might be going. We have a feeling we could be on a motel blacklist somewhere—certainly the motels that don't have plumber's friends handy, but especially the ones that have breakfast buffets. You'd have to ask Tyler about that plumbing thing.

All in all it was five days we wouldn't have missed for anything. We're all looking forward to many more of these trips. Steve and Tyler (quite a bit younger than the rest of us), did raise a concern that will have to be addressed at some point: How long can he and Tyler keep taking these old people out on birding trips? We discussed all-terrain wheelchairs, motorized gurneys, disposable bed pans, and a few other things they need to consider.

Birds we saw on the first day:

Blue Grosbeak, Gray Catbird, Indigo Bunting, White Ibis, Scarlet Tanager, Ovenbird, Wood Thrush, Solitary Vireo, Hooded Warbler, Downy Woodpecker, Prothonotary Warbler, Northern Mockingbird, White-eyed Vireo, Long-billed Curlew, Little Blue Heron, Least Tern, Laughing Gull, American Oystercatcher, Black Skimmer, Royal Tern, Sandwich Tern, Red Knot, Roseate Spoonbill, Willet, Marbled Godwit, Olivaceous Cormorant, Reddish Egret, Osprey, White Pelican, Brown Pelican, Lesser Scaup, Ruby-throated

Hummingbird, Red-winged Blackbird, Pied-billed Grebe, Belted Kingfisher, Great Blue Heron, White Morph of a Great Blue Heron (Great White Heron), Cattle Egret, European Starling, Common Grackle, Blue-winged Teal, Common Moorhen, Sora, Eastern Meadowlark, American Avocet, Sanderling, Ring-billed Gull, Bonaparte's Gull, Ruddy Turnstone, Western Sandpiper, Piping Plover, Black Duck, Mottled Duck, Black-necked Stilt, Lesser Yellowlegs, Northern Shoveler, Semipalmated Plover, Snowy Plover, Summer Tanager, Brewer's Blackbird, Orchard Oriole, Northern Oriole, Swainson's Thrush, Snowy Egret, Mourning Dove, Killdeer, White-faced Ibis, Eastern Kingbird, Northern Cardinal, and American Coot.

New birds we saw on the second day:

Green-backed Heron, Glossy Ibis, American Bittern, King Rail, Yellow Rail, Solitary Sandpiper, Swamp Sparrow, Yellow-rumped Warbler, Barn Swallow, Common Yellowthroat, Rose-breasted Grosbeak, Purple Gallinule, Blue-winged Warbler, Loggerhead Shrike, Blackpoll Warbler, Black-and-white Warbler, American Redstart, Inca Dove, Kentucky Warbler, Fulvous Whistling Duck, Anhinga, Gadwall, Common Snipe, Purple Martin, Northern Harrier, Song Sparrow, Blue Jay, Least Bittern, Wild Turkey, and Tricolored Heron.

New birds we saw on the third day:

Brown Thrasher, Black-throated Green Warbler, Swainson's Warbler, Double-crested Cormorant, Pectoral Sandpiper, Green-winged Teal, Dowitcher, Herring Gull, Chimney Swift, Scissor-tailed Flycatcher, Spotted Sandpiper, Yellow-crowned Night-Heron, Blue-gray Gnatcatcher, and House Sparrow.

Chapter Three

Maybe Cape May

About a week before we were to leave for Cape May I called Steve and asked if he could pick up the van, as he would be the first of us to arrive at Baltimore/Washington International Airport (BWI). "I'll be glad to," said Steve amiably, adding, "I'll also make sure it has a woodpecker guard."

I just don't get it—I run over one woodpecker two trips ago and it's still haunting me. It's not like this woodpecker was endangered or anything. Er, well, I guess *that* one actually was.

Getting back to the van rental. I called the car rental company to arrange for Steve to do the pick-up. After a brief stall, and probably after consulting some black list somewhere, the customer service rep came back on the phone and said they would not be able to let Steve leave the premises with our van because he hadn't made the reservation. They clearly had no knowledge of his fine and upstanding character.

The Family Gathers

On April 30 Lorraine and I flew into BWI. It had been a couple months since I last flew on a 727, and I was amazed, in a painful sort of way, at just how tight the seating was. On my weekly trips to Utah I fly on 767s, and you can actually feel your feet when you deplane at your destination. On this flight I was so cramped that everything below my belt was numb after about twenty minutes.

There's no doubt in my mind that airline seating just keeps getting smaller and more cramped. The width of the seats shrinks and the distance between my seat and the back of the seat in front of me gets shorter and shorter. Now I can see myself getting wider through the hips maybe, but it's unlikely that longer legs account for the loss of leg room. Those responsible for redesigning airline seats are probably moonlighting from the sardine-packaging industry. But as usual, I digress.

When we got into BWI, Steve and Tyler were waiting for us at the gate, and a fine sight they were. The first thing I noticed was how tall Tyler had gotten and how much smaller Steve seemed in comparison.

Steve, employing his superb bedside manner, had persuaded the car rental company to give him the keys to a van. He got one with tinted windows, but we tried not to think about that too much (remember all the "black birds" we saw in Texas). We threw our stuff in, and I endeavored to get us out of the parking garage. Each aisle was designated either a pick-up or a return lane for some car rental company. The exit signs seemed to point in every direction. We finally drew a bead on the real exit and headed off in the right direction.

I have to say, the other passengers in the van weren't much help as they were laughing too hard to be coherent. I felt privileged to be able to supply that much amusement in such a short period of time. But no mind. After all, we *were* here to have fun.

We finally made our escape from the garage and found our way over to the Marriott where Ken, Irene, Ted, and Dorothy were waiting for us in the lobby. After hugs and laughter all around, we stowed all our luggage in the back of the van, put the binoculars and camera equipment out where they would be handy, and drove north toward Wilmington, Delaware.

We hadn't gone 200 feet when Irene asked about the nearest McDonald's. I couldn't believe my ears. They had eaten breakfast "just a while ago." For now we ignored her. However, later in the trip, she often had co-conspirators in the "aren't we ever going to eat?" lobby.

Our first destination was Elk Neck State Park, which occupies a peninsula that juts out into the very northern part of Chesapeake Bay. On the way, several of the inmates started complaining that it was early afternoon already and if they didn't eat soon they might not be hungry for dinner. I started looking for a restaurant.

At the time we were passing through the town of North East. I'm not kidding. The early settlers evidently had very little imagination when it came to naming their town, although there is one school of thought that says the town was named by the first mayor—a compass manufacturer.

Vegetarians in a Crab Place

Anyway, there we were. We spotted an unsuspecting restaurant, parked, and trooped in. As soon as we were seated, menus in hand, we noticed the place was a "crab house." A questionable choice for a group half vegetarian and half anti-crab. Not that we have anything personal against crabs, I just don't like eating things that would eat me if they caught me. The things I eat have to generally be slow, dumb, and herbivorous.

As I mentioned, half the group was vegetarian, so Steve put the menu aside and started asking for an inventory of the larder. Once he'd gotten that, he proceeded to tell the waitress how to make a veggie sandwich that would be to his liking. This was clearly against policy, but she humored him after he mentioned something about a big tip. By the time he was done, she had been instructed to bring him a sandwich on whole wheat with lettuce, tomato, mustard, mayo, cucumber slices, and pickles.

In a misguided effort to make the waitress feel less put upon, Ken, Tyler, and Lorraine said they would take the same thing. Except one didn't want mayo, another didn't want pickles, another didn't want mustard and lettuce, and somebody else didn't want the cucumber. Before all this began, Dorothy had decided on a plain cucumber sandwich on white bread. When Steve heard the words "white bread," he took an immediate interest in her health and insisted that she ask for it on wheat bread instead. To keep the peace, Dorothy capitulated and requested the veggie sandwich as designed by the committee.

By this time the waitress was looking a little wild-eyed and started mumbling about how she didn't like working here anyway. I'm not sure why, but wherever we go we seem to get the fragile waitresses. When all these "exactly-the-same" sandwiches came, a period of passing plates back and forth ensued until everyone was satisfied that they had the sandwich they'd ordered. For a few minutes it looked like a game of Pit.

While waiting for our food, and during its consumption, the conversation ranged from foreign objects found in various bodily orifices to the entrepreneurial possibilities of anti-impotency drugs. Keep in mind that this group has more than the average compliment of medical personnel, so nothing having to do with the human body is sacred. If laughter is as good as medicine, we could have started a clinic right on the spot.

Moving On

A few minutes after leaving the crab place we found Elk Neck State Park, drove to the end of the road, and parked. As we got out of the van and organized ourselves for a hike, Steve and Tyler sprung their first surprise on us. They gave us all T-shirts with "Spady Birding Trip" and the date on the back. Instead of the LaCoste crocodile, on the front, there was a hummingbird. We were very pleased and surprised. It was a great idea.

The next day we all wore our shirts and as we were having lunch, I overheard a couple of guys asking, "What's a Spady?" If they only knew. I'm not sure we do.

We hiked through some dense woods that thinned out as we reached the end of the peninsula. We heard a lot of birds and even saw a few. It was obvious from the get-go that Tyler had the young eyes. The rest of us let him spot the hard-to-see birds and then tell us where to look. Of course we only did this to build up Tyler's self-esteem. It's not that the rest of us can't see and hear just fine, but we feel compelled to let the younger ones carry their weight. At least that's our story and we're sticking to it.

During the latter part of this walk, Ted practiced and perfected his Bobwhite call. He was not quite good enough to lure them out into the open, but by next year I'm sure he'll have Bobwhites following us up and down the trails pointing out other birds to us.

Millville, NJ

After the state park, we crossed the Delaware Memorial Bridge and drove southeast to Millville, New Jersey, where we had reserved a place to stay for the night. I had made the reservations sight unseen, and we were pleasantly surprised at what we found. It was a nice motel. But it was supposed to have a restaurant and that had recently been closed. Maybe they had heard about our quirky ordering at the crab place and just couldn't cope with the veggie sandwich routine. We'll never know.

The hotel desk staff told us that, if we went back up the freeway to the next exit, we would be on the main street of Millville where all the good restaurants were located. This main street must have been five miles long. We drove and drove, rejecting all the usual fast food places, places with dirty windows, places with no cars in the parking lots, places with too many cars in the parking lots, places that had the wrong ethnic menus, places that looked too dark, places that had "family" in the name, and one place that was both dark and advertised not only "real barbecue," but live blues music. Finally, after pulling into several parking lots for closer examination, the group got tired enough to settle on a place, which turned out to be good. Another victory for the committee approach to choosing eating places.

The next morning, just as we were pulling out of the motel parking lot, we spotted a strange goose wandering around looking very much at home on the motel grounds. This goose was nothing like any we had ever seen before. We watched it a while then drove south toward Cape May. It wasn't until later that Ken identified it as a Bar-headed Goose—an Asian species—most likely an escapee from a zoo or some private collection.

Horseshoe Crabs

On the way south we stopped at Heislerville Wildlife Management Area. There we drove up and down the dike roads looking for and spotting a number of birds, but nothing especially new. On the several small beaches there, we did

find an abundance of horseshoe crabs. These are very different from the normal crabs that one finds on a beach. Horseshoe crabs resemble humped, leathery, upside-down food bowls, each with a long sturdy tail sticking out behind. Actually a good place for a tail. If it were sticking out in front, it would probably be called an antenna (just a thought). Unlike most crabs, this crab doesn't scuttle sideways. As this crab moves about on the sand, you can't see any legs because they are all underneath the humped food-bowl shell.

This area is well-known as a beach where horseshoe crabs lay their eggs. It's also well-known to the birds migrating up and down the coast. They stop here and feast on crab eggs until they can barely take off and fly.

Many of these crabs were on their backs, so we walked along turning them over so they could get back to the water. I felt a little uneasy, messing with Mother Nature like that, but I'm not sure she was watching anyway. Besides, she was trying to rain on us. By the time we left, it was definitely coming down hard enough to get things wet.

For the last couple of days before our trip our whole group had been watching the Weather Channel, keeping track of a huge weather front as it moved across the country with the certainty that it would cover the whole Delaware Bay area for the entire weekend. Thinking back on the original planning, I'm convinced it was Steve who picked this particular weekend.

Cape May

A little south of the Heislerville Wildlife area we arrived at the Cape May Bird Observatory's Center for Research and Education—an Audubon center with lots of outdoor bird feeders, a balcony overlooking some swampland, and plenty of books, bird feeders, optical equipment, and other Audubon stuff for sale in the gift shop. They also had a list of recently spotted birds and the best places to find them. In another part of the observatory, on the second floor, was an art gallery. Two bird carvings, one a Yellow-crowned Night-Heron and the other a Kestrel, caught my eye. Both were extremely well done and very pricey. They were still there when we left.

The only problem with the trip so far was that we seemed to be about a week early. The following weekend we would have been there for the World Series of Birding. If we had waited a week, we supposedly would have seen all kinds of birds. But we would also have had to sleep in the van and take a number to step into a decent birding spot.

Now I can just hear you asking, "What in the devil is a World Series of Birding?" Well I can answer that. The World Series of Birding is an event in which teams of birders come to Cape May from all over the country. For seventy-two hours they compete to see which team can find and identify the most birds. Nearly takes your breath away, doesn't it? It attracts a lot of people and is normally scheduled for the weekend the most birds are expected to be present for the festivities. Good thing they don't depend on our family to select the date or there wouldn't be any birds to bird.

During our drive from the observatory into the city of Cape May, the natives in the back of the van once again became restless. We had gone past their feeding time, and they feared for their lives. The first thing we did when we got into town was to stop at a pancake house and have some lunch. As it turned out, this place was only about a block from the motel where we had reservations, so we had breakfast there the next morning too. For us to eat twice at the same establishment speaks volumes for the food and service. Lucky for you I don't plan to add those volumes to this narrative.

Some History

In 1620, a Dutch captain, Cornelius Jacobsen Mey, (sometimes spelled May) explored the Delaware River and named the peninsula Cape May after, you guessed it, himself. Whalers began settling the area in the mid-1600s. In 1761, it became the first seashore resort in America. The city was designated the Cape May Historic District, a National Historic Landmark, in 1976. The city's most distinctive feature is its Victorian heritage, which makes the town very picturesque and interesting. Sitting as it does on the northern point of the entrance to Delaware Bay, the town includes a lighthouse. The first light was established in 1823, although there is mention of a "flash light" at this location in 1744.

Birds are attracted to this cape because of the way it protrudes out into the water. It offers the first landfall for birds migrating north across the bay, and provides a jumping-off place for birds migrating south.

After eating we checked into our motel, a place I had reconnoitered on my check-it-out-trip back in January. It had been closed down at the time, so I didn't get to preview the accommodations, but the place turned out to be okay. Not quite what I had in mind, but close. After check-in, we all moved into our rooms, and I made arrangements to rent a VCR for the evening.

When we got back to the van to head out in the rain, we found Steve dressed in full camouflage gear. He claimed it was intended to keep him dry, but since it made him look like a hunter, it did get some weird looks whenever we asked people where the birds were.

In the city of Cape May there are four major birding areas: The Nature Center of Cape May, by Cold Spring Inlet; Cape May Bird Observatory's Northwood Center, by Lake Lily; the Cape May Migratory Bird Refuge; and Cape May Point State Park. Our first stop, at Cape May Bird Observatory's Northwood Center, netted us several additional places to look for birds. But before doing that, we went out to the Lighthouse area of Cape May Point State Park. This is where they hold the hawk watches, which is when a bunch of people gather for a period of time to count and identify the hawks that fly by. Talk about fun!

We also drove out to the end of Sunset Boulevard, checked out the concrete ship that's half-buried in the surf, tried to spot some birds, and then moved on. It was raining all this time.

Our next stop was the ferry terminal, and then on to pick up the VCR.

By this time we had wasted about as much time as our birdwatching consciences would allow, so we decided to try some of the places we had heard about at the observatory. We drove up the Garden State Parkway and turned east toward Stone Harbor, which is on the Atlantic side of the Cape.

Between the parkway and the beach are tidal ponds and canals that host a number of swimming, flying, wading, or just-standing-around-waiting-for-birders-to-come-by-and-be-amazed birds.

We spent considerable time sitting on the shoulder of the road, watching and identifying, while the traffic whipped by a few inches from my door. It's good the residents of the Cape are used to the vehicular antics of birders.

Once we got to the beach, we drove south and then out to Nummy Island. There was generally plenty of space along the highway to park and observe, and we saw many birds. The later it got in the day the less it rained. By the time we got out onto Nummy Island, it was bathed in sunshine.

It's surprising how much better birding is when the sun is shining. My limited experience suggests to me that even the birds usually know enough to come in out of the rain, which makes them hard to find on wet days. I'd rather not dwell on the implications of why the birds take cover during a rain while the birders remain out in the rain.

Once again we came to the conclusion that we were either a little early or a little late for the best birding, but as Steve commented, "Why should this year be any different?"

Early in the evening, we drove back into town, where we cleaned up and went off to find a place to eat again. We had a place in mind, but it didn't meet all the criteria. Big surprise!

We decided to look for a restaurant in a nearby area of Victorian shops, each unique, known as Washington Street Mall and the adjacent Carpenter's Square Mall. Parking nearby, under (and sort of *in*) a huge bush with pink blossoms, we set off to explore.

After some walking about, we settled on the Pilot House, which seemed to be acceptable to everyone concerned. By this time it had been several hours since we had eaten, which had caused the group to relax their standards a bit. I shudder to think what we would have settled for, if indeed we really had gone a very long time between meals.

Once back at the hotel, we sat and watched a video made during a trip Lorraine and I had taken to the Galapagos Islands a few months before. Surprisingly everyone stayed awake—well, except for Steve, who dozed off occasionally, but came to the surface at crucial points in the showing.

As Lorraine and I were getting ready for bed we realized there was no clock in the room. We couldn't get anybody to answer the phone at the front desk, so we spent the night with one eye (each) on our watches, trying to make sure we didn't oversleep.

In the morning we woke to blue skies and sunshine. En masse we walked down the street and had breakfast at the pancake house. Afterward we drove out to the point again to see if we had missed anything the day before. We hadn't, but it gave Ken and Tyler a chance to climb the stairs to the top of the lighthouse.

The front of the van was still covered with pink petals from the night before. Remember my parking in the huge bush? Steve thought it looked like we had been involved in some strange exotic love ceremony. Not being familiar with exotic love ceremonies, the rest of us had to take his word for it.

While I was inside the video store dropping off the VCR, Ted got into a conversation with a couple of guys who had all kinds of suggestions about where to look for birds. It's amazing how friendly people get when they find out you're a birdwatcher. It's almost as if they think they're dealing with some kind of reality-challenged person. They explain things several times in a louder-than-needed voice, draw pictures in the dirt, and do a lot of pointing and arm waving.

After rounding everyone up, we drove north. We had heard about a place called Reed's Beach, which promised to have some good birding. We found it on the first try. I'm not suggesting that we are directionally challenged, but we *do* occasionally find ourselves in places where we had no intention of being.

We drove along a stretch of beach where we saw a number of Red Knots, Ruddy Turnstones, Sanderlings, and, of course, seagulls. Once we had identified everything in sight, we eased on up along the beach where we found a primitive parking area.

Both Red Knots and Ruddy Turnstones nest in the Arctic during the summer and then migrate south for the winter.

(Just like some people from Minnesota we know.) The Turnstones get their name from their habit of turning over stones to look for things to eat. (Ornithologists are so tricky when it comes to naming birds.) All three of these species—Red Knots, Ruddy Turnstones, and Sanderlings—like to cluster together. Watching them run hither and yon on the beach is like looking at a moving carpet. When they fly, they fly together in one big cloud of birds.

The Birdnappers

As we entered the jetty parking area on the north end of the beach, we noticed a group of people gathered around a wooden viewing platform which overlooked the beach. By the time we got out of the van (which usually took some time), the people had all disappeared. We didn't think anything about it at the time. We walked up to the base of the jetty and followed it out onto the beach, where we started looking for birds.

We were soon met by a young lady who asked us not to come along the beach any farther, as her group was trying to net and band birds. "You can watch from the viewing platform if you'd like," she offered. We retraced our steps and went out to the platform to watch the fun.

The group was busy burying a net in the sand. This net was about twenty-feet square with weights along one edge. These weights were loaded into tubes over explosive charges. The back edge of the net was fastened down at the point of burying. When fired, the weights would go flying up and carry the net with it to cover everything in its path.

Once the net was rigged, the team came back up to the platform where the leader explained to us exactly what they expected to happen. A couple of guys looped around this stretch of beach and then back out to the shore, where they began to haze a flock of birds up the beach toward the net. Those on the platform were in radio contact with the herders.

Talk about hi-tech. The birds didn't have a chance.

The leader explained that when they fired off the net it would inevitably trap some birds in the surf. The group would have to hurry down the beach to help these netted birds out of the water so that they wouldn't drown. He also mentioned they would welcome our help later if we wanted to stick around.

When everything was just right, the birdnappers fired off the net and everyone ran down the beach toward the birds.

We followed close behind. The bird-catching team rescued the birds caught in the water and then covered the entire bird-filled net with a big cloth tarp to shade and quiet their little feathered captives. By this time several of us were helping.

Once the birds were covered, the more experienced folks began to untangle them from the net and hand them off, two birds to each volunteer, for transport to burlap holding-pens up the beach. It was just amazing! Thirty minutes before, we had been watching these same birds through binoculars, and now we were holding Red Knots, Sanderlings, and Ruddy Turnstones in our hands.

At first, the birds were somewhat frantic, but once we had them in hand they calmed right down. We were taught how to put our palm over the back of a bird, with its head sticking out between a couple of fingers, and then wrap our remaining fingers around the bird's wings and body. They seemed to be fairly comfortable in our grasp, and there was virtually no struggling.

The bird-banding team captured a total of 120 birds with that one cast of the net. In addition to banding, they put transmitters on the Red Knots so they could track their migration.

This was a one-in-a-million experience—something that will probably never happen to us again. If you ask anyone in our group what the highlight of this trip was, this will be it.

After we watched several birds get banded, we left the experts to their work and drove north.

Speaking of identifying birds (and digressing again), we were all impressed with the progress Ted had made. On his first birding trip, he was pretty much limited to blackbirds and a few related species. This time he had added the Red-winged Blackbird, several white birds, and a number of others, including the illusive bat-out-of-hell. At the rate he is learning, he should be caught up to the rest of us by next year's trip.

Cream Candy

Speaking of Ted naturally brings me to Dorothy. The whole trip, she kept talking about "cream candy," but it just dawned on me that I never saw any of it. Maybe some background here would help.

Our mother used to make a concoction we called "cream candy." It was delicious—very rich and caramelly. Dorothy was the only sibling who came away with the knack of making it. It's always a real treat when Dorothy brings a batch along or sends us a box, which she is kind enough to do whenever she feels we have acquired sufficient merit. Occasionally, when the back of the van got really quiet, I thought it was because they were just tired or too scared of my driving to talk. In retrospect, it's now clear to me they were probably surreptitiously gobbling up the cream candy. But again I digress. Back to the purpose of our trip.

Our next stop was the Cape May Bird Observatory's Center for Research and Education, the same place we had stopped at on the way south the day before. As I mentioned, a large part of their education program included peddling merchandise to pilgrims like us. To help further the cause, Ted purchased a very nice pair of binoculars for Dorothy; and Lorraine and I got some nice, but pricey, post cards for the granddaughters.

WAWA

As we left, it dawned on the captive passengers that we were headed once again out into the wilderness where there might be a lack of food. Another mutiny was under way, but just in the nick of time we spotted a WAWA. WAWA, for those of you who might not be aware of the finer points of dining in New Jersey, is a convenience store. To our group, who were ready to eat anything (remember, no food for three hours), it looked like gourmet city. And, in fact, it turned out to be okay. We each got a sandwich, a drink, and whatever else we could carry away.

By the time we got into the wilderness everyone was fat, sassy, and ready to spot birds. We drove up Pine Swamp Road, which meandered up through some woods in the Belleplain State Forest. It was a little-used, mostly paved, thoroughfare, so we just eased along. I drove the van while the others walked the road and looked for birds. We could hear a lot of birds and did actually see a few. We had been warned that this was tick season, so the crew didn't feel like bushwhacking, but it was comforting to know we had been able to hit at least one season right.

Take note. Enter any forested area anywhere, and the locals will always claim that it's tick season. According to everyone we talked to the ticks this season were especially bad because of—guess what?—El Niño. And of course the birds were scarce this year because of—guess what?—El Niño.

On the way back to town we drove over to the East Coast of the Cape again to Avalon and then down along the coast to Stone Harbor and out onto Nummy Island again. We got back into Cape May just as it was getting dark.

It was time for food again. We ended up at an Italian restaurant down the street from the motel. The place was crowded and they didn't have a table big enough for all of us, but they did have two tables close together, although one was still occupied. The hostess tried to get some of us to take the empty table right away, and promised to seat the rest of us when the table next to it emptied. They just couldn't seem to grasp that we wanted to go in all together. Finally they gave up and ushered us all into the bar, where we tried to act like we knew what we were doing, none of us being bar habituées. Tyler was allowed to come in with us even though he was underage, but he wasn't allowed to sit down—another obscure New Jersey law.

We all had something nonalcoholic to drink and gobbled up a bunch of trail mix before we finally got our tables. The food was really great and, of course, the company was impeccable. On the walk back to the motel we naturally had to stop and sample the offerings of a candy and ice cream shop.

The Man in the Backwards Pants

We met at the van the next morning for our run to the ferry. We might have gotten away earlier if Steve had not discovered that he had his camo pants on backwards. Now I don't know that we want to dwell on this particular happenstance, and I was encouraged that Steve figured out the backwards pants thing on his own. While several of us were waiting for the others, and before Steve tumbled to the pants thing, Tyler entertained us with an imitation of a skit he had seen on Saturday Night Live the previous evening.

We were laughing so hard that guests of the motel were coming out onto their balconies to see what all the noise was about. Once they got a look at us, laughing hysterically, wiping our eyes, and the big guy with his pants on backwards, their curiosity ebbed and they dived back into their rooms. As soon as we got Steve headed in the right direction, we left for the ferry to Lewes, Delaware.

A red card was included with the ferry reservation. We were to hang it from the rearview mirror so we could be directed into the proper loading lane to wait for the ferry. As we drove past the other cars, Steve waved the red card so other drivers wouldn't think we were cutting in line. The other drivers didn't know whether to ignore him, give him the worm-eating warbler salute (which resembles a peace sign—well at least half of the peace sign), or wait until we boarded and *then* throw him overboard. Our tinted windows apparently obscured just enough of his features to save him once again.

Once safely parked in our slot, we walked into the terminal and picked up some breakfast goodies. We returned to the van just in time to drive onto the ferry. It was a nice sunny day, although a little windy. Ted headed to the bridge to check out the crew first thing, reporting back to us that most likely we would reach the other side without getting wet. The ferry ride was very pleasant.

The Nips Gang

During this trip I discovered, to my dismay, that most of the rest of the group had become substance abusers. The substance they were abusing was that terror of the D.E.A., "Nips®"—a coffee-flavored hard candy. The group was convinced they were getting a buzz from this "caffeine" confection. A careful investigation of the packaging revealed that these Nips had no caffeine whatsoever—just coffee flavoring and sugar. But the offenders weren't convinced. They kept popping their over-the-counter "uppers" like they were candy. Surprisingly, Ken (remember he's the conservative doctor) seemed to be the kingpin at the center of this Nips ring.

We disembarked from the ferry at Lewes, Delaware, and started north toward Bombay Hook, a National Wildlife Refuge on the coast just north of Dover. On the way we poked around in the Prime Hook National Wildlife Refuge. We were pretty much on the clock this day as we had to get Steve and Tyler to BWI to catch their plane at six that evening. We spent several hours exploring Bombay Hook and then left for BWI.

On the way, guess what? The subject of food came up. Again. While I was putting gas in the van, the group trooped next door to another WAWA and tried to buy up enough food to last them for the two-hour drive to Baltimore. Judging from the wrappers and empty bags they left scattered around the van, they succeeded.

After dropping off Steve and Tyler, we checked in to the Marriott and had some dinner. We sat, ate, talked, and laughed—it was a relaxing and fun way to wind up our trip.

The next day Ted and Dorothy, along with Ken and Irene, headed down to Washington, D.C., to see the sights. I watched the news carefully for any untoward incidents involving National Monuments or other tourist locations, but I've seen nothing unusual, so evidently they behaved themselves.

Birds we saw on the first day:

Canada Goose, American Robin, Northern Cardinal, Orchard Oriole, Blue Grosbeak, American Crow, Blue Jay, White-throated Sparrow, Blue-gray Gnatcatcher, Yellow-rumped Warbler, Red-bellied Woodpecker, Tufted Titmouse, Great Blue Heron, Double-crested Cormorant, Common Tern, Northern Parula, Cliff Swallow, Eastern Bluebird, Prairie Warbler, Carolina Chickadee, Brown-headed Cowbird, American Redstart, and Laughing Gull.

New birds we saw on the second day:

Bar-headed Goose, Snowy Egret, Mourning Dove, Boat-tailed Grackle, Blue-winged Teal, Red-winged Blackbird, Willet, Clapper Rail, Common Snipe, Black-crowned Night-Heron, American Black Duck, Black Skimmer, Common Yellowthroat, Barn Swallow, Bonaparte's Gull, American Oystercatcher, Green Heron, Red-breasted Merganser, Great Black-backed Gull, Herring Gull, Western Sandpiper, Gadwall, and White-winged Dove.

New birds we saw on the third day:

American Goldfinch, Killdeer, House Finch, Great Egret, Dunlin, Brant Goose, Black-bellied Plover, Osprey, Sanderling, King Rail, Northern Mockingbird, Mallard, Rock Dove, Mute Swan, Red-necked Grebe, Song Sparrow, Common Loon, Ruddy Turnstone, Glossy Ibis, Red Knot, Turkey Vulture, Ovenbird, Black-and-white Warbler, Greater Yellowlegs, Dowitcher, and Whimbrel.

New birds we saw on the fourth day:

Eastern Kingbird, White-eyed Vireo, Gray Catbird, Black-necked Stilt, American Avocet, Brown Thrasher, Yellow Warbler, White-crowned Sparrow, Downy Woodpecker, Marsh Wren, Tree Swallow, Golden-crowned Sparrow, Louisiana Waterthrush, Rufous-sided Towhee, House Wren, and Rough-legged Hawk.

Chapter Four

As Far As You Can Go

Before I start this narrative I want it known that someone else picked the weekend for this trip. At least that's the way I'm going to remember it. This fact will become important later.

The Family Gathers

Lorraine and I got into Corpus Christi around 3:00 in the afternoon. I walked up to the hotel desk to register and was waiting for some service when who should walk up but Ted. Returning from a walk, he and Dorothy had run into Lorraine in the parking lot.

At this point I must back up to lay some groundwork for what's to come. Earlier in the day on our way south, Lorraine and I had been up the coast in Rockport or Fulton or one of those towns along in there, looking at an oak tree that was reputed to be anywhere from one- to two-thousand years old, depending on what literature you were reading. If tourism drops off, the age of the tree will probably jump to three thousand years.

As we were getting back in the car, our phone rang. It was Steve. He was approaching the airport in Louisville, Kentucky and had just discovered his wallet was missing, although he still had his plane ticket. We were not surprised. Steve has a predilection for some mildly bizarre behavior while trying to meet us. It's almost as if his subconscious is trying to keep him from joining in these adventures. The only unsettling thing about this theory is that we know how bright his subconscious really is.

Steve had been calling everyone he knew, trying to get help finding his wallet. The plan, if it was found, was to send it to him at the place we planned to be the next night. His immediate problem was getting on a plane without any ID other than his smiling face and well-practiced bedside manner. Steve, as you may remember, is a doctor of medicine. Our conversation with him ended with us still planning to meet him at the Corpus Christi airport at the regularly scheduled time, unless we heard from him again. He did call the second time, just to let us know he had talked his way onto the plane (so much for airport security) and would be in Corpus Christi as scheduled. No one had yet located the errant wallet.

We had also gotten a call from Ken earlier in the afternoon saying that their flight had been delayed.

Once all four of us—Ted, Dorothy, Lorraine, and I—were checked into the Embassy Suites, we drove to the airport to meet Ken and Irene, who finally got in around 5:30

p.m. While the rest of the gang was gathering up the recent arrivals, I rented the van Steve had reserved. We piled into our car and the rental van and drove back to our hotel.

After getting Ken and Irene settled, we walked over to an Outback Steakhouse for some dinner.

Mixing Business with Pleasure

During dinner the phone rang. This time it was a business associate calling to say that we (this business associate, another gentleman, and I) had gotten some papers signed, which meant that Lorraine and I, along with these two associates, had just purchased a company in Wisconsin.

This was the first of many calls during the four days we were together, and it became a running joke as the news kept changing every time I got a call. First we had the company, then we didn't, then they said, and then he said, and then we said, until the group must have been tired of hearing about it at all. I know I was. Trying to make something happen in Wisconsin while birding in Texas made me feel rather useless—rather like Reggie, the guy who sterilizes the needles Texas uses to give lethal injections. I have to ask, What's the point? In Texas this is a full-time job, but according to Reggie, it's not a very fulfilling one.

Back to the Airport (the Long Way)

Around 8:00 p.m. we left for the airport again to pick up Steve whose flight was due to arrive at 8:36 p.m. This was our second trip to the airport in the last five hours, and we took the long way to get there both times. Everyone I asked explained that the route was easy, as there were signs all over the place. It wasn't until we were back in town again that we finally tumbled to the fact that the signs with the little hard-to-see airplanes on them and the words "C C International Airport" were actually designed to help us get to where we wanted to go.

I know, it sounds easy now. But at the time it seemed pretty complicated.

In any event, we finally made it to the airport, parked, and walked out to the gate where Steve's plane was supposed to dock. ("Dock"? I'm not sure that's exactly what planes do at a terminal.) The place looked deserted, so we started back toward the main part of the terminal where we bumped into Steve, wearing his safari hat and everything except his wallet. He looked like a birder who was ready to rumble. His plane had gotten in twenty minutes early, and he had been wandering around the airport looking for us, probably hoping he might just be able to escape this adventure after all. I dragged him off to the car-rental place to sign him up as the second driver, but without a driver's license they wouldn't have anything to do with him.

Back at the hotel, we all sat around and watched Steve eat a late dinner that the kitchen kindly put together for him. Between bites, Steve described all the hi-tech gear he had brought this time. Among other things, he had both motion-suppressing binoculars and night-vision binoculars. The poor birds weren't going to have a chance. He had also brought along a Polaroid camera to capture candid shots of the group during the trip.

Heading Out

The next morning we got up, had breakfast, and were on our way by 7:30 a.m. OK, OK—7:45 a.m. Part of the delay had to do with trying to jam into the back of the van all the luggage this group needs to maintain the comfort level we've become accustomed to. Not that it's a lot, but the van had an extra seat way in the back that took up a lot of space we could have better used for luggage.

To start the expedition right, Steve took a picture of me standing on the back bumper of the van with my head inside while I was arranging luggage. About the only thing that the camera could see was the part of me that was hanging out of the van, mainly my backside. When I took exception, Steve shrugged and said, "It just seemed to be a 'Kodak Moment.'"

Ken was also helping load. Someone brought us a heavy rollerboard. Ken and I each grabbed an end preparatory to hoisting it up and over the back seat, but just as Ken heaved up on his end I decided to go do something else. Ken insisted that medical attention was not necessary as the hernia was a small one. Ken and Dorothy were always eager to put their medical skills to work.

The three of us, Ken, Dorothy, I, and our older brother Ed, spent all or part of our growing-up years on a farm, so there were plenty of first aid things to be taken care of. When I was growing up (which was something of a miracle in itself) Ken and Dorothy, both somewhat older than me, were already headed for careers in the medical profession. They were always at the ready to pounce at the first sign of any medical situation that would require them to splint, sew, cut off, apply a tourniquet, poke, feel, or at the very least, give advice. Advice like, "Of course you can pick up rocks with one arm in a sling." Or "So, how does your head feel after that fall? That bad, huh? How many fingers am I holding up?" And then my favorite, "Close enough, let's get back to work."

Why, I remember one time when—well that would be digressing from this birding adventure and I know you don't want me to do that. I think Ken and Dorothy got this medical yearning from Dad who seemed to enjoy taping together the edges of cuts, stanching the flow of blood, applying splints, and performing other first-aid procedures. Anything that didn't call for a death certificate was considered first aid. But again I digress.

The seating arrangement in the van was as follows: I drove, Lorraine was in the copilot seat (or suicide seat, as I heard mumbled a couple times), Ken and Steve were on the first bench seat right behind us, Dorothy and Irene were on the next bench seat, and somehow Ted got stuck sitting by himself on the third bench seat. He never complained about it, and he seemed to see as much as the rest of us. Every so often when he was asked something, or a response of some kind was in order, he sounded like a man coming out of a deep sleep. Maybe he had found a way to enjoy that lone back seat the rest of us had not thought of.

Speaking of "seeing as much," I should give you an update on the level of competence of the two newest members of the group. As you might recall, on their first trip, Ted identified everything as either a "blackbird" or something other than a "black bird." Dorothy's performance got off to a slow start, mainly because she was using the wrong end of the binoculars and/or leaving the lens caps on. Now, however, they are seeing and identifying birds left and right. They've come a long way in a short time. After all, just look who they have for teachers.

The first order of business that morning was a stop at a Walmart, two blocks from the hotel. We needed a step stool for assistance getting into the van—just an example of the adjustments one has to make when traveling with people over the age of—well, never mind. The van was quite high off the ground and some of the passengers needed an interim step to make it easier to board.

"Do the Dew"

After Walmart, we hadn't gone more than two blocks when we had to stop again to let Steve try and find some Diet Mountain Dew. We had been gone from the hotel all of fifteen minutes when he claimed he needed a pick-me-up. The convenience store we stopped at had never heard of diet anything. As we were leaving town I saw one of those signs that advertised "24-Hour Banking." I just don't get it. I don't have that much banking. And I don't have that kind of time.

Our next non-bird-related stop was in Kingsville, where we stopped again to find some Diet Mountain Dew for Steve and fresh coffee for Ted. As before, no one had ever heard of Diet Mountain Dew.

Historical note: I won't do this much, I promise. The land for the town of Kingsville was given to the city by the King Ranch in 1903. They had one-million acres, so a few for a town probably didn't cut into their operations all that much.

Birding at Last

In Kingsville we stopped at the Dick Kleberg Park, part of which is a small lake. This was our first birding stop—other than just pulling off to the side of the road—so we looked at everything several times, relieved to get into the swing of actually looking for something besides Diet Mountain Dew. From there we crossed Highway 77 to the Santa Gertrudis Creek Bird Sanctuary—a little marshy area with a partially dried-up pond. We saw a few birds in the course of our fifty- yard walk.

Back on Highway 77 we had to stop and look more closely at the swallows that were darting around the culverts under the highway. Searching for a place to park, we settled on the parking lot of a little convenience store across the highway. While Ken was checking out the swallows, Steve was—that's right—checking to see if they had any Diet Mountain Dew. In this place they thought maybe they had seen some once.

We each travel with one or more bird books so we can identify most anything by comparing entries in all of them. During the trip Irene left her Stokes bird book someplace, and nothing would do but that we stop and let her buy another one. That's how important an old familiar author is to a birder. We won't speculate on how someone as organized as Irene could lose a bird book in a van.

There are a lot of little towns in Texas that try hard to come up with some claim to fame. Raymondville, the next town we passed through, is no exception. Raymondville is famous for a family that makes boots. In Texas, that means cowboy boots. Their boots are worn by Texas Rangers, cowboys, and royalty, which probably accounts for at least five or six pairs.

From Raymondville we drove east to Port Mansfield, where we hoped to see many new birds in the marsh flats along the Gulf.

But It's a Dry Year...

I might as well explain something right here and get it over with. Because Texas was in about the third year of a drought, we found many dried up lakes, wetlands, and marshes. It was rather disappointing. The result of this drought was that many of the birds we should have seen had the good sense to be off somewhere else. But we were together and having fun. We couldn't see any reason why the birds shouldn't do the same.

Another deterrent to birding on this particular day was the substantial wind. Birds tend to stay hunkered down during windy weather to avoid ending up in another state if they take to the air. Typical of our birding adventures, this was, no doubt, the first and last windy weekend of the year.

On the way out to Port Mansfield I noticed that the check-engine light was on. I'm talking about the van now. Several of the passengers could have had their "check-engine" lights on as well, but I wasn't being paid to monitor their vital signs. I wasn't sure what the check-engine light meant, as all the other gauges were right where they were supposed to be, and the van seemed to be performing within acceptable limits. Nevertheless, that evening I called the rental place and they agreed to have a replacement van waiting for us at McAllen, where we would be staying the following night. They didn't seem too worried about it, so I decided not to fret unless it seized up and stranded us along the road.

At Port Mansfield the marshes were all dried up and there was very little bird action. We did stop in the city park to use the restrooms. Beside the door to these facilities was a prominently displayed sign which read: "Watch for Poisonous Snakes." For some reason most of us decided that another half hour would not make that much difference. However, it wasn't a total loss. We did spot a couple of wild turkeys wandering around in the vicinity.

On the way back into Raymondville we saw a Couch's Kingbird. I know this is so exciting that you'll want to see one for yourself right away, but please don't try this without the aid of a professional like one of us.

In Raymondville we looked for a place to eat lunch and found a small Mexican restaurant. It was not one of your typical Tex-Mex places. It was authentically Mexican, and the food was excellent. I had a hamburger, but the others apprised me of the quality and flavor of what they were eating. I tried the salsa and pronounced, "These people know what they're doing!" Secretly I thought of asking for the recipe for my glass-etching friend back in Fort Worth.

By the way, Raymondville has an elevation of forty feet, so if the polar ice caps melt during this warming trend that some people think is happening, this restaurant will soon be under water. If you want to try their food, you'd better get there sometime in the next ten thousand years. Just a word to the wise.

So far on this day, I had gotten several calls from my business associates in Wisconsin letting me know that what we thought we had last evening was not the case anymore and asking "What should we do about it?"

Before we left Raymondville, Steve finally found some Diet Mountain Dew. That freed up a lot of time for birding that day and I'm guessing for the rest of the trip. From then on we all endeavored to make sure he had an ample supply.

Laguna Atascosa

From Raymondville it was a short drive to Laguna Atascosa National Wildlife Refuge. This refuge sits along the western shore of Laguna Madre. On the other side of the lagoon is South Padre Island. The Refuge is one of the hot birding spots in the United States. It was very dry here also. We stopped at the visitor center and then took a walk on one of the trails. Seeing nothing there except grackles and one Green Jay, we took the seventeen-mile drive around the refuge. It was still very windy. At the visitor center we were told to look for an Aplomado Falcon, which naturally looks like two dozen other species of falcon, except for two feathers which make it quite distinctive—unless it is a juvenile, a female, or is molting. The Aplomado Falcon is rather rare in this country, so of course we had to see it.

The place where there was supposed to be a lake was just dry, cracked lake bed. The seventeen-mile drive around the Refuge was somewhat uneventful. However, at one point we saw a large bird fly across the road in front of us and land off to our left, behind a small ridge of grass. We identified it as a Crested Caracara—a large, striking-looking bird which lives mostly on carrion and can be seen in southern Texas although it is mainly native to Mexico.

No sooner had it landed, than loose feathers started flying over the top of the ridge of grass. Another Caracara had joined the first one. Clearly they were eating, or at least plucking, something which had started out with feathers. One or the other would fly up and around then settle back down to help with the dinner preparations. With the sun low in the west, the light on these two birds was optimal for showing off their red, white, yellow, and black coloring. After some time, one of them took off carrying what turned out to be a seagull. They flew off to a more remote spot, probably to finish their meal in private.

Further along this refuge drive, near the place where people had been spotting the Aplomado Falcon, we were scanning everything that moved—which wasn't much. At one point a couple of falcon-looking things flashed by us. The moment I stopped the van, all the doors burst open, and we piled out with gear in hand. We ended up down the road a ways, having seen only a Black-shouldered Kite. Lorraine and I, sitting in the two front seats, had been sure the leading bird of the twosome that flashed by us was the Aplomado Falcon, but we never found it.

As we turned back, we saw our van sitting in the middle of the road with all its doors standing open and the motor running. We agreed that it could only be there for one of two reasons. It had either held a group of birders who thought they had seen something exciting, or it had harbored a group of illegal border crashers who had just spotted "*la migra*" (the Border Patrol).

We never did see the rare falcon. Back at the visitor center we took a three-mile drive out to a large lake. The water line, which used to be right up next to the viewing platform, was now three hundred yards away. There were lots of birds, but they were all way out there, impossible to identify in silhouette against the sinking sun. In all we managed to see sixty-three different birds that day.

After Laguna Atascosa we went on down to the City of South Padre Island and found our motel.

The Motel from Hell

I had made all the lodging reservations for the whole trip. For four of the nights I had gotten us into Embassy Suites, which is usually dependable in terms of quality and cleanliness. This was the only night I could not get us rooms in the Embassy Suites. I had called all the resorts on the Island and found them to be very expensive for just one night's stay. In the interest of fiscal responsibility, I had settled on the Lagoon Motel (name changed to preserve anonymity).

On the Internet I had seen an inviting picture of the motel overlooking the lagoon, so I requested rooms on the lagoon side. We would be able to watch birds right from our rooms!

But when we got there, we found that the place was not on the lagoon, but only on a little canal. It looked nothing like the picture. I took a copy of the picture with me into the office and asked the desk clerk to explain. He studied it for some time. "Yeah," he said, "that's what the hotel probably looked like thirty years ago, before the area was built up."

Our reservations were all scrambled, but the clerk finally got us four rooms on the canal side of the motel. Several blocks of houses, condos, apartments, hotels, and what-not blocked any view of the lagoon. It was late, we were hungry, and we just weren't mentally ready for this, but we went ahead and checked out our rooms.

In Steve's room, water was cascading down one wall. He didn't know whether to mention it or not, in case a waterfall would make his room more valuable. None of the first four rooms was satisfactory, so the desk clerk moved us all to other rooms. (I almost said new rooms, but there was nothing new about this place.) As we entered the office, another guest was there complaining that he had run a bath but was unable to turn off the water. You're right. His room was right above Steve's. The whole place was a disaster.

We finally got unloaded and left to find some dinner. Because I had to make a couple of phone calls, I asked Ted to drive. In no time he was initiated into the perpetual chorus of "Watch out, that's one-way," "There's a stop sign," and "Watch out for that pedestrian on the bicycle."

We pulled into one place and all traipsed in only to find that they were closed. We couldn't imagine why. It was only a little past nine.

We pulled into another likely looking establishment, only

to see through the windows that they had plastic table cloths and no customers. Suddenly we couldn't eat on plastic table coverings? This is apparently a more upscale group than I thought.

We finally ended up at a place called Blackbeard's. Blackbeard's was great. I had one of the best burgers that I've had in a long time, and I don't even remember what the table surface or covering was.

That night in the scummy motel passed without anyone dying, although a couple of us were sure we would. No one balked at leaving early in the morning. There was no need to go around and roust them out of their roosts. Everyone was waiting at the van when Lorraine and I came down from our second-story mold factory.

Our next project was to find a place to eat breakfast. Steve insisted on a place that could serve us really fast, so we could get out there finding birds. We finally settled on a place, but Steve was still grumbling about the time this would take out of our day. And then, suddenly reversing himself, he proceeded to order two breakfasts. Remember that Steve was still traveling without the aid of any money whatsoever. He was depending on the largess of—well—*anybody* to keep him fed, housed, and supplied with Diet Mountain Dew. This was an unusual position for Steve as he is usually loaded with funds and very generous. He took to this moneyless situation alarmingly well.

We knew that Ken would be going strong all day because he had grits for breakfast. Personally, I have always been of the opinion that anyone who would eat grits would comb a goat with his teeth, but in this part of the country grits are regarded as manna from heaven.

Sabal Palm

We finally got on the road and ended up at Sabal Palm Audubon Sanctuary, which has the best-preserved Sabal Palmetto (also known as Cabbage Palm) forest in the United

States. It sits right on the United States/Mexico border—as far south as you can go in Texas and still be in the U.S. Normally it's full of birds, except when extraordinarily dry, as it was at the time of our visit. Normally it looks like a jungle, but now most of the grasses and small shrubs were dry and puny. Between 8:00 and 10:30 a.m., when we were there, it was already getting very warm. Despite the unusual dryness, the birding wasn't all that bad. We did see twenty-three different bird species while there, thirteen of which we hadn't seen the day before.

It was here at Sabal Palm that we had an extended discussion about whether we were seeing a Reddish Egret or a Little Blue Heron. Steve had been seeing red on everything all morning. I think it was the Mountain Dew.

Sabal Palm is adjacent to Brownsville, the site of Fort Brown (originally Fort Texas, re-named for its commander, Major Brown, after he died defending it from a Mexican attack). It was built by the Americans on Mexican territory. It's funny how touchy some countries can be when you try to liberate even a little part of their land.

It was also right near Brownsville that a group of Confederates captured a bunch of Yankee soldiers one month after the Civil War had ended. Given half a chance they'd do it again today. All this background, by the way, was provided by the people at the Brownsville Convention Center and Visitors Bureau.

Down in the Dumps

On the way back to Brownsville we decided to stop at the city landfill. Lorraine and I had tried this on a previous trip, but couldn't get in because part of it was on fire. This time we pulled up to the gate, and I was elected to go in and see if we could bird the dump. "Bird the dump"—now there's a phrase you don't hear every day. This sounds a little weird—okay, a lot weird—but it's the only place along the Rio Grande where Mexican Crows (aka *Tamaulipas* Crows) reside.

The guy in the gatehouse knew exactly what I wanted and gave me a printed map with directions. People and vehicles were coming and going through this gate, with the U.S. Border Patrol checking every vehicle that was coming out. The Border Patrol had collected a group of suspected aliens who stood under a tin roof waiting to learn their fate. We drove in and followed the "Birding people go here" signs to a spot overlooking the face of the dumping area. It was covered with birds and, sure enough, we saw Mexican Crows. They look so similar to American crows that you have to listen to the call, which of course is in Spanish. Just joking. Actually, how could we tell they were Mexican Crows? The book says there are no American Crows at this dump. So much for birding expertise.

On the way out of Brownsville, the group nearly mutinied when they got the idea I wasn't going to stop at the Visitors Bureau. I don't know how or when they decided that this little band of travelers was a democracy. But I decided to humor them. Once they had coerced me into stopping, they pressed their advantage by insisting that I park in the shade, which meant that I had to pull the van up on the sidewalk crosswise to the marked parking spaces. Fortunately there were very few cars in the parking lot at the time. Once I got the van parked, I discovered the urgency was due to too much water, coffee, and/or Mountain Dew, coupled with too few rest stops.

The Great Texas Coastal Birding Trail

On the way to the Santa Ana National Wildlife Refuge (hereafter referred to as Santa Ana), we made two stops along the Great Texas Coastal Birding Trail.

You may remember from our eastern Gulf Coast trip (Chapter Two), that the great State of Texas has identified all the coastal birding places from the Louisiana border on down the Gulf coast to the Mexican border and then up the Rio Grande to—well, I'm not sure how far it goes, but how far into the interior can you go and still call it a "coastal" birding trail? Anyway, there are maps and information on it which we picked up at the Brownsville Convention Center and Visitors Bureau.

We followed directions to the first stop after several turns that landed us in the front yard of someone's farmhouse. We had turned around and headed back toward the main road when we noticed a gazebo-like viewing structure on the edge of a small lake off to our right. We found a little track heading out across a field in the right direction. We bumped along it all the way to the gazebo. And guess what was on the other side of the gazebo? Why, a paved road of course.

The gazebo overlooked a small lake which was about half the size it would have been with normal rains. As we approached the gazebo, both Lorraine and I spotted an Anhinga just swimming out of sight on the other side of it. Along with some Roseate Spoonbills, we saw many cormorants, which Lorraine and I kept trying to turn into Anhingas. We never saw that elusive Anhinga again, and the rest of the group thought we were imagining things, for which, I must insist, there was absolutely no historical precedent. None.

As we prepared to leave this spot, Steve asked me to move the van, as the side door was in some tall grass. He had been attracting chiggers, and he had no desire to accumulate any more of them. High grass and low shrubs are where they seem to hang out, and he was of the opinion that they were gradually working their way up his legs. He had serious concerns about their final destination.

Our next stop was a Methodist campground. As it was on the list of birding places, the staff was accustomed to people just driving in and asking where the birds were. They were very helpful about pointing us in the right direction. Of course good church people would be interested in pointing people in the right direction, wouldn't they? We spotted an Inca Dove and we think a White-tipped Dove as well. It was a most appropriate spot in which to find a bird symbolic of peace and love.

By now it was late in the afternoon and the group had not eaten since breakfast. We stopped at a fruit stand to pick up some apples and bananas, along with one jicama for the group to sample. It was not the best jicama that Lorraine and I had ever eaten, but no one else in the group had tasted one and had nothing to compare it to. They scarfed it up in no time at all. We hoped it would keep us going until we could get some dinner, which would have to wait until it was too dark to see birds.

Santa Ana was somewhat of a disappointment. Again, everything was very dry. The lakes were almost nonexistent, and the birds were few and far between. We hiked the trails through the wooded part of the refuge, and then explored the trails out around the large ponds—or what *should have been* large ponds. They were now mostly dried up.

In this area we did see numerous Scissor-tailed Flycatchers and a pair of Black-bellied Whistling Ducks. These ducks are beautiful with their red bills and black, white, and rusty wings; a rusty chest (the rust color is the real color, not just from being around water); and black belly; grey head; and almost-red legs and feet. They are easy to spot and identify.

Part of this trek around Santa Ana was a loop trail that paralleled the Rio Grande River for a quarter mile or so. There were numerous trails coming up from the river to meet the trail we were on. We couldn't think of any reason someone would be going down to the river along here. On the other hand, to folks who might not want to use a bridge and have their luggage or documents checked by the Border Patrol, crossing the river here might make more sense. There were signs at the beginning of this riverside trail warning us not to walk it alone, as it was an area of considerable illegal drug activity. Unfortunately, as hard as we looked we weren't able to see *any* activity, neither drugs nor birds.

By the way, Santa Ana Refuge was not named after Antonio Lopez de Santa Anna, the Mexican general the Texicans threw out of this part of Mexico. I'm sure you're all relieved.

McAllen

After Santa Ana, we were off to McAllen and our hotel. But before we could do that we had to stop at the McAllen Convention Center to watch the evening return of the Red-crowned Parrots. According to local intelligence, the parrots love to hang out around this building. I'm not sure why, as there are no statues—oh, sorry, that's *pigeons*. Once again we lost out. The parrots were supposed to show up around dusk, but dusk came and went, and no parrots.

Meanwhile I stayed in the van trying to make contact with the local Dollar car rental people to coordinate the switching of vans. Remember the problem with the check-engine light? McAllen is only a town of around sixty-thousand people, so to expect to find a phone number for a local car rental agent might have been a little much. Finally, in desperation I called the national office, which turned me over to their handler of suspicious people. "All our new vans have the same problem," he told me. "Just ignore it." I had been doing just that for a day and a half, so I agreed to keep it up.

Eventually, the parrot pursuers gave up, and we went to check in at Embassy Suites. On this day we saw twenty-eight bird species that we had not seen the day before.

Checking into the hotel turned out to be a bit of a hassle. They just couldn't quite get their heads wrapped around the idea that the reservations were for four Spadys, one of whom was a Naiman, and that one of the Spadys was paying for two Spadys. (Remember Steve and his missing wallet?) Steve was lucky his dad was along to bankroll him. We finally persuaded them to put us all on the same floor.

Once we got ourselves settled in, we went out looking

for a place to eat. While waiting for the parrot pursuers, Irene and Ted had spotted what looked like a good eatery, so we tried it first. It was called Republic of the Rio Grande. It took us twenty minutes to get a table. Then it took another twenty minutes to get waited on. We had to tackle a busboy to get water and iced tea after the waiter seemingly ignored our requests. Finally he showed up with more water and iced tea, amazed to find that we had not waited for him. Although the service was lousy, the food turned out to be very good.

All during dinner, Steve kept trying to shame the rest of us into an earlier start the next morning. It worked, but he only gained us about twenty minutes worth of extra time. It was a very small return on the investment of time and energy he had put into it.

Anzaldúas and Beyond

In the morning we drove out to Anzaldúas Park, which is just south of Mission, Texas—another place listed on the Texas Birding Trail. This park sits along the Rio Grande too. On the levee between the park and the river there were a number of large portable lighting units and some Border Patrol vehicles. I figured the lights were not there for night birding.

As we pulled into the park, we saw another van parked alongside one of the roads with a group of birders off to one side looking up into a tree. I pulled up behind it and Steve and Ken bounded out. Steve tried to sidle inconspicuously up to this group to find out what they were looking at. Now Steve is six-foot-four with blond hair—what's left of it anyway—and hard to miss. It was like a moose trying to blend in with a flock of sheep. The rest of our group was busy trying to convince me that I should not park behind the other van, as it would look like we were trying to join their group. Which of course is exactly what Steve and Ken were trying to do.

Anyway, trying to act like I had at least a modicum of birding etiquette, I pulled our van up the road a ways and parked under a tree. I started to get out of the van when I noticed Ken and Steve standing behind the other group, waving their hands and using all sorts of body language to try to tell me something.

At first I thought they were attempting to fend off the chiggers that must have finally reached a more sensitive area of Steve's person. If we had been playing baseball I would have assumed their signals were meant to encourage me to steal first. I looked around to see if I was in danger of being caught in a longhorn cattle stampede, but all was quiet on the bovine front. I finally guessed that they wanted me to move the van again, which of course I did.

Once I got the van situated in an acceptable spot, Steve and Ken came over to explain. They were laughing so hard they could hardly stay upright. It seems that this bunch of birders was an international group being led by some local, whiz-bang birder. He had brought them out to this park to see a Gray Hawk which was that very moment nesting in the very tree under which I had parked. The other group was rudely wondering out loud what kind of idiot was driving our vehicle anyway, commenting on my parentage, and planning the disposition of my earthly remains.

Steve and Ken were in the grip of such hysterical laughter that they could hardly gasp all this out to the rest of us. Their laughter was highly contagious. We were all slapping our thighs and staggering about, with tears running down our faces. This other group of birders watched us for a minute then made a beeline for the farthest corner of the park, casting frantic glances over their shoulders. We figured they must have seen something awfully interesting to have headed in that direction so abruptly.

We spent an hour or so in this park and saw a Rose-throated Becard, a Tropical Parula (sounds like some kind of poisonous snake, but it is a warbler), and a Nashville Warbler. After a while, we did actually get mingled in with a couple of other birdwatching groups, so we were all able to help each other spot and identify birds.

As we returned to the van, we could see the Gray Hawk still sitting on the nest. Either this hawk was accustomed to plenty of action under its tree, or it had been glued there by the local Chamber of Commerce.

On the way from this park to our next stop, I accidentally ran over a quail dashing across the road. The others in the van didn't notice this distressing occurrence, and I hesitate to even include it in this journal since I'm still getting hassled about the Acorn Woodpecker I ran over in Arizona a couple of trips ago. I'm afraid the family will get the idea that I don't really subscribe to their reason for these expeditions.

On our last trip through this part of the country, Bentsen-Rio Grande Valley State Park had been one of the highlights, birdwise at least. The Park had been full of campers, and the occupants of each campsite had put out all kinds of goodies to attract birds. The birds had taken full advantage of this largess. This time, when we pulled into the park we noticed there were very few campers. As we walked around, we realized there were very few birds as well.

No sooner had we gotten started on our walk than the Gray Hawk group pulled in and started walking the park right behind us. The leader of the group had apparently forgiven me for my earlier indiscretions and seemed glad to point out to us an Orange-crowned Warbler and a Northern Beardless Tyrannulet. From the name of that last one you'd think that surely there must be a southern version, or at least a bearded version, but there isn't. Why this poor little bird got tagged with such a long moniker is a mystery.

We walked and drove the roads of the park and saw very little more. We were either too late or too early, and that, along with the drought, made for a disappointing bird count. By now it was coming up on lunch time, and the group was tending to get a little testy about the lack of feathered flying things.

We settled on Rio Grande City as the town we must not leave without getting something to eat. It looked on the map to have the largest population of anything in our vicinity. We drove through town on the one-way highway and, seeing nothing encouraging, turned around and started back on the one-way Main Street. That's when we spotted a Mexican restaurant. Ted and Irene, who had successfully led us to a good place the night before, challenged us to do as well for lunch today and flat out refused to take any responsibility for picking a good place again on this trip. We pulled into the parking lot and filed inside.

The place was really old. In fact, Robert E. Lee might have eaten there while serving at Fort Ringgold after the Mexican War, before he left to defend his home state in the War of Aggression by the Northern Hordes (or, as Northern textbooks refer to it, the Civil War). The walls were covered with old stuff from shovels to pictures of bandidos. Our first clue about what lay ahead should have come when we realized we were the only customers in the place.

Before we could sit down, several of us had to help Ken unzip the stuck, back-pocket zipper of his cargo pants. We gathered around his backside, fumbling around with his pants. The impression this gave the restaurateurs might have been misleading. All I can say is, the next time Ken gets a stuck zipper, we're going to take him out in the woods to fix it and not try it in a public venue.

We finally sat down at a table, trying not to look too closely at the conditions around us. No sooner were we settled, than Irene, thinking that in some way she was helping the males in the group, started commenting on the anatomy of our waitress. Why she thought we would have noticed this girl's...ah, well, never mind. We finally got her off that subject and on to looking at her menu—that is, the parts of the menu she could see between the food samples encrusted on it.

Ken took a turn at the restroom and came out looking a little pale. He had encountered a large cockroach and a sign that said, "Please don't wash your hands, they're already cleaner than anything else around here."

South Texas humor is a little different for sure, but in my opinion that sign crossed the line in a big way. Steve volunteered to go in and drive out the cockroach. I'm not sure what he had in mind, but it was probably hi-tech. Sure enough, when I used the facility later (not until I had finished eating—I didn't just fall off the tamale wagon), the cockroach was in the hallway, lying on his back, gasping his last.

We finally ordered and waited for the food to come. Everyone else at the table got served except me. My chicken *chimichanga* was still some time in making its appearance. As the others were scarfing up their food (hurrying to get out of there), there was some banter about catching, executing, and plucking one of those scrawny chickens out back. That set the tone for my taste buds right then and there. When the *chimichanga* finally came—well I'll have to describe it. It was a big mound of something in the middle of a big plate all smothered with orange stuff. Nothing was visible except melted cheese. I gingerly poked into the mound and, sure enough, there was a *chimichanga* in there. However, the chicken was not quite done. I took a couple of bites and put my fork down. I would have returned it to the kitchen, but by this time my appetite was gone. The cook had accomplished what a description of the bathroom and the general ambience had failed to do.

As we left, we had a good laugh. Steve made the comment that these trips were like "bowel day at the nursing home—a great release." I hoped he was referring to the laughter.

We stopped at Falcon Dam, looked around, and hiked about half a mile down a hot and dusty road. The return trip seemed like two miles. We also drove over to, in, and around

Falcon State Park. Once again, there were very few people and fewer birds. We did see a couple new ones nonetheless—a pair of Pyrrhuloxia, a Forster's Tern, and some Black Skimmers.

Exiting the park, we pointed the van back toward Corpus Christi. Between the park and Hebbronville we saw Crested Caracaras all over the place.

Falfurrias

From Hebbronville we went to Falfurrias, famous for its Don Pedrito Jaramillo Shrine. The locals tell the tale of Don Pedrito, a Mexican faith healer born in Jalisco, Mexico, who they say was cured through faith and given the gift of healing in a vision. He came to Los Olmos Ranch in the late 1800s, and for twenty-some years thousands of people flocked to him to be cured. I felt better just driving through town.

In Falfurrias we again went in search of a place to eat. We spotted a drive in, pulled in, made some uncomplimentary remarks about their menu offerings, and left.

Leaving town, I knew I would have to make a right turn at an upcoming intersection, but I was behind a large truck and couldn't see ahead. I was in the middle of the intersection before realizing that I should have turned. At the urging of someone in the van—I'm not sure who it was—I turned anyway. I turned into the far left lane of the two lanes coming toward me, swung around behind a lady sitting in the nearest of the left-hand lanes waiting for the light to change, and then on to the right-hand side of the road again. My passengers volubly, if shakily, yelled something about seeing their whole lives pass before their eyes. At least it kept their minds off food for a good ten minutes.

The next town of any size was Kingsville, on Highway 77. My companions, in ominous language, let me know that we would categorically not leave this town without eating. Luckily we quickly spotted a pancake house. As we waited for our food, the strangest conversation sprang up. It started with Irene complaining about all the porn that was showing up on her computer and the fact that she couldn't seem to get rid of it. Then it moved on to a proposal that we should all get telephone video capability on our computers so we could see each other when we talked. Dorothy observed that Ted would have to put on clothes before getting on the internet. (Nobody asked for any further information on that.) Then Steve chimed in with the question, "If that happened, how would we be able to tell it from the normal porn we're now getting?" From there the conversation was just headed downhill. Thank heaven our food arrived.

When we finished our dinner, we were all preparing to settle up with the establishment when Steve put a very generous tip on the table. Where in the world did he get the money? Ken came along and picked up Steve's generous tip and left a more modest one in its place. "Why'd you do that?" Steve inquired indignantly.

"It's my money you're being so generous with," Ken explained. For some reason we all found this hilarious. It had been a long day and was now around 9:30 in the evening. I'm not sure that's a good excuse for our merriment, but it's the only one I've got.

Back to Corpus Christi

We drove the rest of the way into Corpus Christi and got ourselves re-settled in the Embassy Suites, but not without a struggle. Two couples had to ask to be moved because of bad plumbing, dirt, and various other issues.

The next morning we were up, had breakfast, and took Steve to the airport. This time we followed the signs and took the shortest way without any trouble. I'm not sure why we found it so difficult before.

For some inexplicable reason Steve didn't want all of us traipsing into the terminal to watch him leave. However Ken and I went far enough to make sure he was going to be able to get on the plane (remember the lost wallet). When it became evident there would not be a problem, we left to get in some more birding.

Our plan for the day was to work our way up the coast to Aransas National Wildlife Refuge and then back down to Corpus Christi.

Our first stop on the way north was at the Connie Hagar bird sanctuary. Connie Hagar was a woman who moved her family to the Rockport area and, during her lifetime, became a world-class birder. Well, at least a Texas-class birder. And of course if you're from Texas, the World and Texas are synonymous.

In Search of the Painted Bunting

Our next stop was Goose Island State Park. This park sits on the coast and extends inland to include the camping area, so there are water birds, shore birds, and inland birds in attendance. One bird that we had been looking for on this trip was a Painted Bunting. So far it had eluded us. But according to the Park people on this day, Painted Buntings had been seen in the camping area within the last couple of days.

Side Note: At the start of our trip, on our way from home to Corpus Christi, Lorraine and I had stopped at Goose Island to check out the birding. The park had experienced a fallout the day before we got there. That figures. There was probably a fallout the day after we were there too. (If you need to refresh your memory about fallouts, go back to Chapter Two.)

So our group canvassed the shore and water birds first and then parked in the camping area to take a hike through the woods. I was wearing cut-offs, so my legs were bare from the knee to the top of my socks. As we stopped to watch a bird, I looked down and saw about two-dozen mosquitoes on each bare leg. They were thick and aggressive and gave us a lot of incentive to keep moving.

Alas, plenty of mosquitoes, but no Painted Buntings.

Aransas Wildlife Refuge

At the Aransas National Wildlife Refuge Visitor Center, we were told the same story we'd been hearing along the entire coast: the Whooping Cranes were gone for the season, it was very dry, and there were hardly any birds around. We decided to bird the whole area anyway. Our first stop was at Jones Lake, and even though it was partially dry, there were a lot of birds. There were also several alligators chasing each other around the pond with malice aforethought. Or maybe they were just feeling amorous. With alligators it's hard to tell.

We climbed the observation tower, but the wind was blowing so hard that the only creatures foolish enough to be out and about were us. The sixteen-mile drive around the refuge yielded nothing more than a view of a javelina family.

On our way back to Corpus Christi we stopped at another birding area. It was just a strip of island a hundred yards or so out in a small bay covered with birds of all kinds—spoonbills, both White and Brown pelicans, egrets, and herons, just to name a few. Ken had his scope on them and was rattling off names left and right. It was the first and last time on the entire trip that we encountered a plethora of birds in one spot.

As we drove back through Corpus Christi we stopped at Hans and Pat Suter Wildlife Refuge. This park has a boardwalk that crosses the marshes right to the edge of the Bay.

There were numerous birds, and it was a great culmination to our birding adventure. The Gulf was the only place we visited where the water levels were normal.

After we got back to the hotel, we drove down the street and had dinner at Macaroni Grill—a nice relaxed and fun way to wind up our trip. I talk a lot about birds and birding, which is our excuse for these trips. But the main reason for these excursions is to be together and share a whole year's worth of laughter.

The next morning we said good-bye to Ted and Dorothy, loaded our own stuff into the Town Car and Ken and Irene's stuff into the van. Then we drove both vehicles out to the airport. Again we managed to take the correct route. We dropped off the van, said goodbye to Ken and Irene, and headed home, thrilled to have survived another birding trip with the family.

At some time in the future I would like to introduce our kids to the fun we experience on these trips. I'm not sure how we would handle the logistics of the thing, but it's something to think about.

Birds we saw on the first day:

Ruddy Turnstone, Willet, Purple Martin, Double-crested Cormorant, Northern Harrier, Couch's Kingbird, Brown-crested Flycatcher, Golden-fronted Woodpecker, Great Blue Heron, Green Jay, Northern Mockingbird, Greater Roadrunner, Osprey, Loggerhead Shrike, Sandwich Tern, Tricolored Heron, White Morph of a Great Blue Heron (Great White Heron), Reddish Egret, Caspian Tern, Rock Dove, Great-tailed Grackle, House Sparrow, American Kestrel, Mourning Dove, White-throated Swift, Red-winged Blackbird, White-tailed Hawk, Eastern Meadowlark, Scissor-tailed Flycatcher, Killdeer, Common Snipe, Mountain Plover, European

Starling, Blue-winged Teal, American Coot, Glossy Ibis, Ruddy Duck, Northern Shoveler, Ladder-backed Woodpecker, Lesser Scaup, Belted Kingfisher, Harris's Hawk, Cattle Egret, Green-backed Heron, Snowy Egret, Dowitcher, Black-necked Stilt, Turkey Vulture, Red-bellied Woodpecker, Black Vulture, Cave Swallow, Cliff Swallow, Wild Turkey, Brown Pelican, Herring Gull, White Ibis, American Crow, Horned Lark, Lesser Yellowlegs, Crested Caracara, Black-shouldered Kite, Vesper Sparrow, and Whimbrel.

New birds we saw on the second day:

Brewer's Blackbird, Laughing Gull, Bobwhite, Long-billed Thrasher, Plain Chachalaca, Little Blue Heron, Pied-billed Grebe, Common Moorhen, Great Kiskadee, Least Grebe, Northern Cardinal, Summer Tanager, White-eyed Vireo, Tufted Titmouse, Hooded Oriole, Gadwall, Buff-bellied Hummingbird, Mexican Crow, Bonaparte's Gull, Roseate Spoonbill, Anhinga, Inca Dove, White-tipped Dove, American Avocet, Western Sandpiper, Mottled Duck, Black-bellied Whistling Duck, and Altamira Oriole.

New birds we saw on the third day:

Blue-gray Gnatcatcher, Black-throated Green Warbler, Pyrrhuloxia, Forster's Tern, Black Skimmer, White-winged Dove, Eastern Kingbird, Gray Hawk, Rose-throated Becard, Tropical Parula, Nashville Warbler, Orange-crowned Warbler, Northern Beardless Tyrannulet, and Bronzed Cowbird.

New birds we saw on the fourth day:

Royal Tern, Eared Grebe, Common Loon, and White Pelican.

Chapter Five

I'll Have a Quetzel—por Favor

Before this trip there was a flurry of communi-cations. Ken called to see how we were doing. When Ken found out that the guide had lost his bird scope, he decided to take his along. "That's OK, Ken," I joked. "The guide's probably only a couple weeks away from cataract surgery." We had a good laugh.

Dorothy and Ted had emailed the day before to let us know how excited they were to be leaving for Miami in the morning.

Steve called to let us know he and Angie were ready and excited. With the exception of Ted and Dorothy, we all planned to meet in the terminal at Dallas/Fort Worth International Airport (DFW). Ted and Dorothy would meet us at our destination.

So what was all the excitement about? We were leaving on a ten-day birding trip to Costa Rica. If you don't find that exciting, you'd better just skip to the next chapter.

From Hardship to the Lap of Luxury

Before I launch into this narrative, I have two things to get out of the way. The first is an apology. I'm not sure to whom, but an apology nonetheless.

I've been party to something that can't be undone and which may have changed the tenor of our birding trips for all time.

In the past we've arranged our own transportation, our own lodging, our own meals, invented any historical significance for the places we've visited, and identified birds on our own. We've become toughened from eating cheese-covered armadillos in places that still had sun-bleached squares on the door where the owners had just recently—and momentarily, because they saw us coming—taken down their Health Department closure notices.

We've stayed in dives that couldn't attract a cockroach, and rented vans with tinted windows that skewed bird colors by a couple degrees, overheated, made weird noises, and came without a driver. We've driven our own vehicle and scared ourselves out of our wits on the road (to say nothing of the astonishing new vocabulary I learned from backseat drivers).

We've gotten lost and seen far more back roads and downtown areas than we had on our itinerary.

We've schlepped our own luggage in and out of hotels, motels, and hovels of every description and wondered what in the world we were looking at through our binoculars as we frantically pawed through our bird books in a desperate attempt to determine whether what we thought we saw had any relationship to what was actually available to see.

All this had turned us into a lean, mean, birdwatching machine. By the end of the trip to Costa Rica, that would all change. It may take years of hardship for us to toughen up again—if in fact this group ever will consent to return to our old rough-and-tumble birding ways. For my part in all this, I do apologize. I will not mention it again—maybe. Why this group's expectations and preferences are about to undergo a change will soon become clear.

They "Failed" My Test

Before leaving on this trip, I painstakingly researched all the birds we might see in Costa Rica and made up a bird list for each couple to use in keeping track of our sightings. I also included two spurious birds, just as a test mind you, to see if the group was paying attention.

My list contained 881 birds. During the trip, Jonathan (our guide) told us that the very latest official count of bird species in Costa Rica was 879. In the end, not one of the group claimed to spot the spurious birds. I had offered a $50 reward for anyone who could spot even one of them. I still have my $50 and, come to think of it, I may even have forgotten to mention the reward. So much for trying to trip up anyone in this family of intrepid birders.

I've included the official sightings list at the end of the chapter and in the appendix.

The Clan Gathers

Ken and Irene had flown into DFW on Thursday, one day earlier than the rest of us, and had stayed north of the airport, where they took the opportunity to visit that evening with a nephew and his family. The next morning Ken called and asked if we would pick up a prescription for him. He had sprained something playing basketball with the nephew and his kids—we never did find out just what. He needed something to alleviate the pain.

At DFW Friday morning, we all endured the screening, probing, and patting that go along with getting on an international flight, or actually any flight, these days. With their focus on things like nail clippers, emery boards, hair spray, and other items that have a long, disgraceful history of being used in violent terrorist acts, the U. S. Transportation Security Administration (TSA) has trouble getting people through the system. But we can all sleep—or fly—easier knowing terrorists have been denied the tools of their trade.

We found Irene waiting at the gate. Ken wandered in a few minutes later. They had caught a glimpse of Angie heading into a restroom, but she hadn't been seen since. No one had seen Steve at all.

There had been a gate change, so Ken and I decided to walk down to the old gate to make sure Steve and Angie weren't waiting there. Sure enough, we found Angie at the old gate with a pile of luggage. But still no Steve. Angie had no idea where he was. In the airport yes, but exactly where, no one seemed to know.

Angie whipped out her cell phone and called him. About that time a phone in her carry-on bag started to ring. "That's Steve's phone ringing now," she said as she rummaged around and found it, mumbling something unintelligible about blonds.

Not long after, Steve came strolling up. He had been out looking for the bird book recommended for Costa Rica. Now this might seem a natural thing to do since we were going birding; however, he had, or thought he had, already bought the book, but he'd lost it. (How do you lose a bird book anyway? Maybe by leaving it at the ball game? The opera? The art museum? Or maybe by sewing it up in a patient? Remember, Steve's a doctor.) In any event, it had disappeared. Knowing how this group works when identifying birds, he didn't want to be in the position of not having his own reference material.

Not surprisingly, none of the bars, pizza joints, yogurt palaces, or pretzel emporiums in the airport seemed to be selling Costa Rican bird books.

A New Addition

Let me say a word here about Angie—a new name to readers (besides the participants in this little adventure, there must be two or three of you now). Angie is the newest member of the family, having married Steve last December. She got sucked into birding with us because I'm guessing she didn't know enough to exclude it from the marriage contract. I will cut through all the suspense here and just say that she acquitted herself with honor and some dignity—although that may be a little strong. She became very good at spotting birds—and spas.

Health and Other Stuff

While I'm on the subject of participants, I might as well bring you up to date on the rest of the group.

Lorraine, because of a fall down some stairs (I was ten states away at the time), was struggling with a bad back and neck. Irene was still having problems with her knees. We've already mentioned Ken and *his* self-induced trauma. Steve was looking fit, except for forgetfulness and losing things. Ted and Dorothy had no complaints to speak of, which speaks volumes for clean living and upright thoughts—Ted's email jokes notwithstanding. I was feeling fine too, although for some reason the sight of me triggered in Steve an idea for a new male urinary-incontinence product.

The group as a whole was about as fit as we've ever been at the beginning of one of our expeditions. But to be safe, we had all purchased travel insurance so that, if we got into any kind of medical trouble, we wouldn't be at the mercy of "Our Lady of Hope for the Best Hospital and Grill." (Not to belittle the medical sophistication of Costa Rica—which is world-class.)

Once we got Steve and Angie moved to the right gate, we sat around trading expectations, ideas, and news of Costa Rica. It was still two hours until flight time.

Steve told us about a jungle viper that was so deadly a person would hardly have time to say "pass the cheese" before going on to that great cheese market in the sky.

Ken asked, "Have you all taken your vitamin B shots?" We all looked rather blank until he explained that bugs don't seem to like people with vitamin B oozing out of every pore. We allowed that we hadn't. "Well, the bugs will be clinging to you like a wet burnoose," he replied, giving us something new to worry about. Evidently the bugs in Costa Rica have some kind of built-in vitamin B detector.

Steve assured us he could take care of any and all medical emergencies, as he had in his med-bag an assortment of pills, vials, syringes, tourniquets, and one miniaturized gurney (just in case we had to wheel a sick frog out of the jungle), constipation remedies, diarrhea remedies, and vomiting remedies. He had us covered coming and going. It was quite comforting that he'd actually remembered to bring it.

This bag of goodies was properly checked onto the plane, but when he opened it after arriving in Costa Rica, he found that all the bottles of pills had been opened and dumped in the bottom of the bag. Gotta love airport security.

Dressed to the Nines

During our wait, the ladies got to discussing our clothing situation. Most trips we men just pick stuff out of our closets that we think won't embarrass our wives too much. But for a trip into the humid jungles of Costa Rica we had to have special stuff. Companies that equip suc—sorry—

customers like us, make a cloth that is supposed to "wick perspiration away from the body" and "dry in minutes after being washed."

I've always been of the opinion that perspiration evaporating off the skin is what keeps us cool, and yet here I was, heading into the hot humid jungle, wrapped in cloth that was going to keep that from happening. As for "drying in minutes"—well we'd just have to wait and see, wouldn't we? The final irony was that anything made of this cloth was super expensive.

I can buy a pair of shorts for under four dollars at any thrift store in the country, and here Lorraine was buying me shorts for forty dollars a pair. Steve should be getting into *that* instead of this male urinary-incontinence thing. During the trip I had so much water being wicked away from my body that I felt like I was walking around in my own little cloud.

Eh?

A couple of times during this conversation and the resulting laughter, along with all the other noise in the terminal, Ken and I had a bit of a problem hearing comments from the other end of our row. Steve accused us of being hard-of-hearing. He advised everyone else that if Ken and I encountered a snake not to shout at us, but to throw something to get our attention. At least I think that was what he mumbled. Everyone hooted with laughter. Ken made the excuse that he'd just had his ears drained, drilled, and dried, or some such thing. I couldn't come up with of any excuse for my purported condition.

Got Gummies?

As time passed, someone demanded to know where I was keeping the Gummy Bears. I had, in the past, made the mistake of supplying the group with what they considered to be too-small quantities of this gooey confection. Ever since, I've been expected to keep a large supply on hand in case anyone in the group had an urge to feed a seagull or loosen a filling.

Angie swore there was a candy store close by, so the two of us hiked a long way down the terminal until we found it. Sure enough, they had Gummy Worms and Gummy Bears, so I purchased as much as we could carry. But when we turned back toward our gate, Angie pled urgent business elsewhere and disappeared. By the time I got back to the others they were no longer in the mood for the stuff, so I had to carry it around Costa Rica for the next ten days, ending up bringing much of it back to Texas.

We finally boarded our flight and found ourselves all sitting in one row across the plane. There were six of us and exactly six seats. The airlines refer to this as "problem containment."

Viva Costa Rica!

The four-hour flight was uneventful. We had a good meal and more leg room than one usually gets on these flying toothpaste tubes. We arrived in Costa Rica several hours after sundown. The San Jose airport is in a suburban area seventeen kilometers outside of San Jose proper. I had been seated in a window seat, and getting out of that seat after four hours made me feel like a walrus trying to get out of a wet bathing suit.

After clearing immigration, we found a lady holding a sign that said "Spady." She steered us through customs after which we were met by two other people who took our luggage and guided us to our bus.

As we were being driven into town and to our hotel, our guide (the sign lady) explained what we would have seen if it had been light: "That out there is a coffee plantation. That over there is a pineapple field." Everything outside the bus was as dark as the inside of a cow. But she was pleasant and helpful and wanted us to feel the experience.

The Hotel Bougainvillea in San Jose, where we spent the first night, was very nice. As soon as we arrived we met up with Ted and Dorothy. Check-in was swift and, after settling into our rooms, we gathered in the bar and got acquainted with what was to become habitual—fresh fruit drinks and world-class coffee.

Before returning to our separate rooms, Steve and Angie took us to their room and passed out T-shirts and wind breakers with "Spady Costa Rican Bird Quest" and the date, along with a large, colored Quetzal on the back. The words "Costa Rican Bird Quest" were wrapped around a small Quetzal over the heart in front. We wore them with pride.

Morning found most of us up at first light, out walking around the gardens. In addition to its beauty, the area had its share of birds. At seven we gathered for breakfast, where we met our guide for the trip, Jonathan Sequeira Barboza, and our bus driver, Manuel H. Salas Araya.

The food was great and most typical of what was to come—breads, a variety of fresh fruits, eggs, pancakes, waffles, hot and cold cereals, sausages or bacon, and of course fresh fruit juices and coffee. We didn't have all of that at every breakfast, but always significant portions of it, done very well and presented elegantly. It was a far cry from our usual raiding of motels' Danish-and-milk-or-coffee "Continental Breakfast" bars and then running for the van.

Jonathan and Manuel would eat all their meals with us, which gave us many opportunities to ask questions. Each morning they briefed us on what to expect that day.

Off We Go—in Style

After breakfast our luggage was loaded *for us* and we all climbed into our bus, which was large enough to accommodate about twenty people. Along with the luggage, we carried a large ice chest full of bottled water, soda, and snacks—even raw sugar cane at one point in the trip.

With only ten people in the bus, including our driver and guide, we could each have our own window to hang out of, if we wanted. Jonathan sat up front with the driver, where he had a PA system at his disposal anytime he needed to talk to all of us. It was a great way to go, and you will begin to see what I meant about not being able to get this group back to our old style of birding.

Before leaving the parking lot of the Bougainvillea, I got everyone's attention and explained to the family that, early in my negotiations with International Expeditions and before they would actually consent to taking us on as a group, I practically had to promise that this group would treat their driver more respectfully than they had treated their previous driver. There could be no yelling of panicky directions, name-calling, mumbling, praying out loud, grumbling, curling up in a ball on the floor sucking their thumbs, claiming they were seeing their lives flash before their eyes, or any other deviant behavior. Feigning absolute ignorance of what I meant, they finally agreed to behave themselves. It even worked for a couple days.

Our bus ride this day took us from San Jose over the pass of the Cordillera Central, a volcanic mountain range, and down into the lowlands to the town of Siquirres. From there we would travel by boat.

But I'm getting ahead of myself.

Sloths, J.C. Lizards, and Even Birds

The trip over the mountains was amazing. We saw hundreds of different kinds of trees and bushes in addition to ferns, flowers, and all sorts of other growing things. It was the end of the dry season, so even though the forest looked very verdant to us, it was not as lush as it would be in a couple of months. At one point we saw a couple of coatis in a tree, and in one small town we stopped to gaze at a Three-toed Sloth, also up in a tree.

Now sloths don't come with a lot of warm, fuzzy, huggable qualities. They never groom themselves, so as they get older they look progressively grubbier. It gets so bad that they can become host to plants, fungus, and who knows what all else growing in their hair.

This sloth was sitting in the crotch of a tree completely unconcerned with our comments on his hygiene. Steve was convinced it was stuffed and nailed in place so guides could show it to people like us. It was a sad-looking specimen. But what sloth isn't?

We saw a few birds as we traveled over the mountain range, but mostly what we saw were miles and miles of heavily forested mountains and deep valleys. Jonathan was on the speaker telling us about Costa Rican history—the people, the politics, and anything we might be seeing—or just answering questions.

This is where we saw our first J.C. Lizard. "J.C." stands for Jesus Christ. I know it sounds irreverent, but the lizard is so named because it walks on water—standing up on its hind legs and running across the surface on large, spread-out toes held up by surface tension. Of course this only works for the lizard as long as it keeps moving. Otherwise it sinks just like anyone else.

Early on we learned that both Manuel and Jonathan were very good at spotting things along the road. If Jonathan saw a bird, he could tell us what it was and where to find it in our five-hundred-page bird book. (Each couple had a copy of the book Jonathan had recommended for Costa Rica and he seemed to have it memorized.)

Our usual procedure is to see a bird and start trying to decide what it is. We discuss and second-guess and then either take a vote or decide to go with whatever we haven't seen yet—all this in an area where we're rather familiar with what we're looking at.

Using this process in Costa Rica however, where nearly every bird was new to us, we would have spent most of our time pawing through our books trying to find out what we had seen, while a dozen other species fluttered around trying to get our attention. Looking back now, I can't imagine trying to bird Costa Rica in such a limited time-frame without the services of a knowledgeable guide.

Toward the Caribbean

As we descended from the mountains onto the lowlands, we started to see banana, pineapple, coffee plantations, and Brahma cattle grazing in open pastures. Everything was very green and quite lush.

I use the word *plantations* because that's how Jonathan and Manuel referred to them. Some of them did have large fields, but most of the plantations consisted of a couple of acres behind a house. The housing in this area was quite basic and somewhat primitive compared with what we had seen in and around San Jose.

We also started to see more birds and were continually shouting out "Stop!" "*¡Alto!*" "Oh oh oh!" "Hey hey, look at that!" any time we spotted something new and exciting.

After about four hours, we pulled up to a marina in Siquierres. Manuel started unloading some of our luggage onto a small boat.

A word here about Manuel. Manuel was—how should I say this?—very effusive. Look it up. I don't want any misunderstanding. Manuel was a hugger—very friendly to everyone, but especially the ladies. He was always so glad to see us, gladder than we were to see ourselves most of the time. He was a good traveling companion.

We had each packed two sets of bags—a small one to take on the boat and the rest to keep on the bus for later in the trip. Manuel promised to meet us at the airport in San Jose on Monday morning. We'd be flying back across the mountains in two small chartered planes. I didn't much appreciate the way he crossed himself when referring to this plane trip.

Jungle vs Forest

We took off upstream (or maybe it was down—I'm not sure). It wasn't exactly a thrilling whitewater run. It was probably all of six inches above sea level with no gradient at all. We would traverse four different rivers getting to our destination: Tortuga Lodge in Tortuguero. The rivers were brown and varied, from thirty to two-hundred yards wide, lined with mostly forest/jungle.

"What's the difference between a jungle and a forest?" you ask.

A forest is, according to my dictionary, a "dense growth of trees and underbrush covering a large tract." A jungle, on the other hand, is "any impenetrable thicket or tangled mass of tropical vegetation." Having boated and hiked through this stuff, I can't in all good conscience say that most of it was an impenetrable thicket, but it sure came close to being a tangled mass of tropical vegetation in some places. So I'm afraid we were in forest most of the time.

"I just got back from a week in the jungles of Costa Rica" has a much better ring to it than "I just got back from a week in the forests of Costa Rica." Shoot, I can walk five minutes from my house and be in a forest. But from now on we'll call these accumulations of flora and fauna "forests." Just remember they were far more exotic than anything we'd seen in the good old U.S. of A. Especially after paying . . . well, we don't need to go there.

It just seems that when you have monkeys and jaguars in the forest, it should be called a jungle. Right? But I won't belabor the point any longer. Forest it is.

Tortuguero

Back to the river. After a time, we tied up to a little rustic dock, unloaded the ice chests, and had lunch on a picnic table in the yard of a Tortuguero National Park building. There were several other boats there belonging to fishermen who were taking a siesta. The lunch that Jonathan and Manuel had brought from the hotel was very good. The sun was shining, and we could see the surf where the river met the Caribbean. Behind the park building there was a colony of huge yellow, black, and white Golden Weaver spiders. Serious creepy factor for any arachnophobes among us.

We had one moment of real excitement on this boat trip when Angie saw something close to the boat and gave out with a shriek that scared up birds for some miles around. What looked like a crocodile turned out to be a partially submerged log.

Our boat captain during this trip, and during our entire stay at Tortuga Lodge, was Walter. Walter was not only good with the boat, but was a skilled spotter of birds and animals. He was also the mayor of the town of Tortuguero.

Tortuga Lodge sat on the west bank of a river that was maybe two hundred yards wide. The east side of the river was separated from the Caribbean by a strip of land maybe as wide as the river. Immediately across from the lodge stood a big tree which served as the terminal and northern end of the runway for Tortuguero Airport. At the southern end of the runway was the town of Tortuguero, population about 600.

The lodge faced the river. It had gardens behind it and beyond the gardens lay the forest. It boasted a nice pool, dining room, and all the amenities except for glass on the windows of the guest rooms. At first we thought the lack of glass was a small oversight. The room Lorraine and I had was on one end of a group of rooms, so we had screens on three sides of our room, nearly reaching from corner to corner, which allowed us to feel, hear, and smell the outdoors. Outside one set of windows was a pond abounding in birds, frogs, toads, and a small caiman (think "crocodile" minus the steroids).

We were given time to settle in, and then we took another boat ride up one of the small tributaries of the big river that flowed past our lodge. These tributary rivers were sometimes as narrow as twenty feet wide, and at times, what with one obstruction or another, offered just enough room for Walter to get the small boat through. We would ease along, looking for anything that might be interesting. We saw birds; white-faced, howler, and spider monkeys; crocodiles, caimans, turtles, and frogs. We only saw one snake, but it was a good one. It was a bright yellow Eyelash Viper lying on a big leaf hanging over the edge of the water, supposedly the most deadly reptile in Costa Rica. We left it as we found it.

These river excursions were great. Jonathan would hear a bird, tell us what it was and where it was going to be, help us spot it, then tell us on which page we could find it in our books. This was birding as it was meant to be. Once again you can sense my concern for ever getting this group back to birding the old way. On our next trip they'll want someone to hold and focus their binoculars.

That evening we had dinner in the dining room. During each meal, the cooks would ask what we would like for the next one. They would suggest several choices of entrees, and once we reached a consensus, they would serve it family style at the next meal, along with vegetables, soup, and other great things.

After dinner we sat and talked. Several of the group took a dip in the pool. Then we all turned in and were lulled to sleep by the night music. Jonathan had warned us to ignore any blood-curdling screams we heard in the night—it would just be owls flying up and down the river searching for prey. It must be a good way to prevent tourists from participating in any revolutionary activities before morning.

The night music included entertainment by frogs, toads, and monkeys. You'd think that frogs couldn't make that much noise, but they are truly raucous. Each frog comes with its own repertoire of sounds, joined by the sound of howler monkeys in the jungle—excuse me, forest—two hundred feet away from us. Of the three species of monkeys known in the area, howlers are the largest, and they sound quite intimidating. Some of the night noises sounded like barking, screeching, and something like someone repeatedly and rapidly pounding on a hollow log. They added immensely to the experience.

This had been our first full day in country, and we had seen at least fifty bird species—most of them new to us. That's a very good day. As always, Lorraine was busy keeping track of our sightings in her little book.

Sunday morning we were up at 5:30 and met Jonathan at 6:00 in the gardens to look for birds. We saw several Montezuma Oropendolas—large birds, mostly chestnut/purplish with bright yellow down the side of a long tail, blue and pink facial skin, and a bill tipped in orange. They were a striking sight sailing around among the coconut palms and other trees in the garden. These birds weave a hanging nest about three feet long.

I promise I won't launch off into detailed descriptions of every bird that grabbed me, but this one was something else. It turned out to be quite common, so we got to enjoy it often.

We also encountered our first poison-dart frog in these gardens. The one we saw was very small, red with black legs. We would see several other kinds of poisonous frogs before the trip was over. They are not all that deadly, but their poison has been used by native hunters to slow down game and allow them to get up close and personal.

Jonathan did mention that if we ever ate a poison-dart frog by mistake, we should have emergency medical help standing by. I'm not sure why he thought he needed to give *this* group that warning. Nothing about our demeanor up to this point could possibly suggest we'd just up and eat a poison frog. He hadn't known us long enough to draw that conclusion.

Tortuga Lodge was at the end of everything. We had come about twenty-five kilometers on the rivers, within a kilometer or less of the coast, and it was another thirty-four kilometers up to the mouth of the Colorado River (*Rio Colorado*), where the next closest town, Barra del Colorado, is located. There was only one other small group of guests in the lodge, and we seldom saw them, except during meals. We pretty much had it to ourselves.

Tortuguero National Park

After breakfast we piled into the boat for another three hours of meandering through the forest via a narrow stream. On the way we stopped and picked up our permit to enter Tortuguero National Park. We saw several quite rare birds, including the American Pygmy Kingfisher and a Tiger Heron. Again we saw several troops of monkeys.

Jonathan had warned us when traveling in the forest not to reach out and touch or grab things like vines, leaves, or flowers. Snakes often look like vines. They also like to sun themselves on leaves, some of which are as big as a Kentucky Derby hat and may be the same color as the snakes. Bright flowers attract bugs. Bugs attract lizards, birds, and frogs—and guess what they attract? You've got it, snakes. Most of these snakes are shy and will slither away from humans, but they won't hesitate to strike if threatened. Jonathan was equipped with a snakebite kit just in case. He had never used it, but for the kind of money we had forked out, they had to make the trip sound exciting.

During this particular excursion, Irene asked Jonathan if anyone was growing marijuana out in these forests, and if not, why not, and could they if they wanted to, and if they were, how would they get it out. She sounded like an advance scout for the Spady Cartel looking for a new supplier. Jonathan's response was rather noncommittal and vague. I don't think he took her seriously, and I was afraid to ask how serious she actually was.

Another word about Jonathan. He has a Doctorate in Plant Analysis, speaks five languages, including Russian (which has nothing to do with his knowledge about local drug connections—maybe).

Throughout the morning we saw numerous butterflies, particularly the large, electric-blue Morpho and another that is electric blue on top and bright yellow underneath.

When we got back to the lodge, several of us went with Jonathan for a hike out into the forest behind the gardens, while the rest of the group elected to stay at the lodge and try out the swimming pool. In the forest we heard many birds, but couldn't see them in the dense, second-growth forest. The overstory pretty much blocked out the sunlight, leaving the forest floor below rather dim. We could hear howler monkeys close by, but we couldn't see them either. Their noise—sort of a bark/grunt that starts low and grows in volume and intensity—is unnerving if you don't know what it is.

Over a lunch of rolls, fresh salad, fresh vegetables, tuna steak, and pasta, Jonathan told us more about the people in this area of Costa Rica.

After lunch we had some time to ourselves. I wrote in my journal and then took my camera out into the gardens. A few of the group napped while others just wandered around.

Early in the afternoon, we climbed back in the boat and headed up another river to do some more exploring. We again saw howler monkeys and White-faced Capuchin monkeys, some with babies clinging to their backs. We also saw a number of new birds and many more butterflies. The blue-to-brown water, green reeds and sedges, tropical flowers, and the forest, made our trip very beautiful and peaceful, and colorful as well.

Birding the Easy Way

So far we'd only been at this for a day and a half. It's amazing how fast even a bird-watching purist can succumb to a life of ease and indolence. I'm referring here to Ken, who is the one who has to carry around a forty-pound scope just so he can make sure one white feather in some bird's tail can be picked out and identified. Well, not really picked out. That's a poor choice of words. Spotted is what I meant.

Ken is the one who has to look up each bird in his own book to verify we got the identification right.

Now, as we boated up this little river, he would sweep his arm toward the forest and say, "What's that?" expecting Jonathan to come up with the name, an imitation of the call, and the page number in the bird book. And Jonathan better not take too long at it either. I have to admit the rest of us were not far behind in sliding down the slippery slope of dependence on a hired expert.

Before returning to the lodge, we docked in the town of Tortuguero. We walked up the main street—a dirt path between the back doors of two rows of houses. As I mentioned earlier, the town sits on a strip of land maybe two hundred yards wide, with one row of houses facing the river and another facing the Caribbean. The buildings were poor-looking by most standards, but the people were clean and nicely dressed. The landscape was much cleaner than some other tropical and near-tropical places we've been. The people were friendly but not pushy. In other countries Lorraine and I have visited, everyone was peddling everything from family crafts to family members.

We stopped at a local craft cooperative and bought some things, including postcards and a small notepad made of banana paper for Lorraine.

At dinner that evening we dined on squash soup (which even *I* liked), quail, potatoes, and several other dishes, all done to perfection and looking glad to be there. Well, one of the quail looked a little grumpy, but what could you expect?

After dinner everyone except Lorraine and I went for a swim, flagrantly flouting the one-hour rule in spite of the fact that most of them were medical people. What's this world coming to?

While the others were swimming, I took a flashlight and tried to spot frogs and toads in and around the little pond next to our rooms. Later we learned that these musicians of the murky waters were responsible for most of the night noises we heard while we were there. It was a relief to discover that all those horrific sounds came from something too small to eat us.

At this lodge, our towels and wash cloths were folded like swans, sailboats, or flowers, and left in the center of our beds. Several other places we stayed presented linens in the same way. Terrycloth origami.

On this trip we didn't once have to find our own way around—geographically speaking. We didn't have to find restaurants, choose from a menu, find our own lodgings, or figure out what birds we were looking at. I've come to the conclusion that taking out the unpredictability—the trauma brought on by having to do these things for ourselves and the feeling of elation when we succeeded—is what I remember as the high points of previous trips. Not that this trip wasn't fun, mind you. It was just different.

Before dinner each evening, we were offered a variety of appetizers that included fried plantain patties, olives, dips, and cheeses. Just a little something to get the digestive juices flowing. It worked very well.

Monday morning most of us were up and out by six. As I shaved, I stood looking out our back screen watching the hummingbirds harassing the flowering bushes just inches from my face and the Montezuma Oropendolas gliding by, all in the bright sunshine of a new morning. Some of the time I was shaving and looking through the binoculars at the same time. It was so exciting that I didn't want to miss any of it.

Out in the garden we found a couple of men banding birds. These fellows had a mist net set up out in a clearing and had caught a number of birds. They were part of some "Worldwide Geo-something-or-other"—a seven-month study of migration patterns. (Or maybe they were just a couple of locals hired by the lodge to give the tourists something to talk about.) We watched until we were summoned to breakfast.

Taking Flight

After another great breakfast, we loaded all our gear into the boat and crossed the river to the airport terminal. Remember the big tree? There we found two six-seater, single-engine planes waiting for us. The pilots divided us up and got us wedged in. They put Lorraine, Dorothy, Ted, Ken and me in one. "Who's liable to cry?" asked our pilot. I thought he said "Who wants to fly?" so I raised my hand and he had me ride shotgun. Apparently I was his backup if his old pacemaker gave out again. Flying didn't look so hard to me. Besides, Ted, who's been taking gliding lessons, was sitting right behind me. We were in good hands.

It was fascinating to catch a bird's-eye view of the lowlands and coast, with all the forest and winding rivers we had boated around in and on spread out below us. We flew over farms, ranch lands, and banana and pineapple plantations. As we started to climb up over the mountains we flew into the clouds which obscured everything until we descended a few miles from San Jose.

Waiting at the airport was Manuel, who was very glad to see us. He had the bus all stocked and was ready to roll.

The Road to Fire Mountain

As we left the airport, Jonathan explained to us that rice growers in Costa Rica were upset because the government had agreed to import cheap rice from another country. In protest, these growers were closing some of the roads around the country. He mentioned that he had warned us so we would know, if we seemed to be traveling in a circuitous route, it was because Manuel was bypassing these blocked roads. How he thought we would have any idea whether a route was circuitous or not, I do not know.

Our first stop of the morning was a craft cooperative in Sarchí. The town is famous for its large colorful ox carts. If you've seen any travelogues or travel literature about Costa Rica, you've seen gaily and intricately painted ox cart wheels, many as high as six feet tall. We browsed the shop and everyone purchased a few items. It had all the regular tourist stuff, along with some fairly nice furniture. They also sold—surprise, surprise—many carry-away sizes of the painted ox carts.

As soon as we were back in the bus, Irene got into the snacks. To keep her from feeling embarrassed, we all joined in and soon had everything licked clean.

No sooner had we finished noshing than we pulled into a restaurant for lunch. It was perched on the side of a hill overlooking the Central Plateau of Costa Rica. The food was good and the view went on forever. As was our newly acquired custom, most of us ordered a fresh fruit drink. A very good one was called "soursop" (*guanábana* in Spanish). It tasted like a cross between grapefruit and pineapple, but not too tart. It was served with either water or milk. I didn't get up the nerve to try one with milk, but someone described it as a sort of runny milkshake.

After lunch, we climbed back into the bus and went only a short distance before stopping in the town of Zarcero to look at a church and its gardens. It was quite unique. The gardens had many shrubs shaped like double arches, all in a row leading up to the entrance of the church. Scattered around the grounds were many other topiary shrubs clipped in the shapes of animals, some of which we recognized and some of which seemed to have sprung from the fevered imagination of the clipper, looking uncannily like the work of Edward Scissorhands.

The inside of the church was very colorful, but not gaudy. Out in front of the church were two stone angels guarding the entry into the sanctuary. In the best tradition of European statuary, one of the angels had a broken wing.

The next leg of our journey took us up through the town of La Fortuna and around Arenal Volcano. The road was very curvy, with lots of ups and downs. The going was slow, but the scenery was spectacular.

The Family Geriatric Business Plan

During this drive we got to discussing, once again, how we were going to handle the aging population of this group in the future. We decided that, because of all our experience in traveling with the aged (I don't know why they were all looking at me), we should be able to monetize this knowledge and open our own travel agency—"Geriatric Travel, Inc." That settled, the discussion veered off to how we could make money dealing with the decreased bladder capacity or outright incontinence of this same segment of the traveling public.

By the time we finished, we had developed the concept and part of the marketing campaign (okay, a few slogans) for a product that would be a giant leap ahead of any currently available adult diaper in its technical practicality and social sensitivity. I won't go into any more detail. First, we don't want a competitor jumping ahead of us on this. Second, you'd probably think we're crazy—or at least crazier than you thought before. When we start looking for investors we can't have anyone thinking that!

Cow Guts

Before we arrived in La Fortuna, Manuel brought us to an abrupt halt along the highway. Jonathan jumped out and went across someone's yard and had a word with people we guessed were the owners. Jonathan then waved us over to look at some very strange-looking flowers. They resembled the stomach and intestines from a cow.

You may ask, "How would you know what the stomach and intestines of a cow look like?" And I would reply, "I grew up on a farm full of cows and they all had stomachs and intestines. Occasionally we would butcher one, which was a high day indeed, and I got to see what all the inner workings of cows looked like." Any more frivolous questions?

It was a strange plant but not completely unpleasing to the eye, cow guts notwithstanding.

Mt. Arenal—the Fire Mountain

As we approached La Fortuna, we could see the cone of Arenal Volcano rising out of the otherwise somewhat flat landscape. It's only 5,357 feet high, but because of the lack of foothills it looks much higher. Arenal is a very active volcano. Most of the lava flows down the west side. On the east side the cone is covered with trees and other vegetation.

We arrived at Montaña del Fuego (Mountain of Fire) Hotel and Spa, which is composed of a number of individual units, called *cabiñas*, plus dining room, office, spa, and swimming pool. From our front door we could look directly at the west side of the mountain—maybe two miles away. Out our back door, which had a small balcony, we looked out over a valley lush with grass, scattered trees, and bushes of various sorts, many of them flowering. The opposite side of the valley was covered with lush grass about halfway to the ridge where the trees started. It was breathtaking.

After checking in, we boarded the bus and drove to the

dam that creates Lake Arenal, the largest lake in Costa Rica. The country has very few lakes, so it's not like there is a lot of competition. But not to belittle Lake Arenal, it's about twenty miles in length. It would be a big lake even in Texas.

From the dam we took a dirt road up along the lake and then got out to walk up the road until it got too dark to see birds. We spotted a lot of new birds.

As we searched for birds, we noticed the mountain was making sounds like distant—and not so distant—thunder. It was explained to us that the mountain makes three basic noises: "whoosh," "boom," and "ka-boom." "Whoosh" and "boom" are innocuous. However, if we were to hear a "ka-boom" and were still alive, "we should take note of which way the natives are running and give serious thought to following them."

During this birding session, Ted, Dorothy, and Irene came up with the idea of a life list of birds they had been close to, but hadn't seen. Since they were standing in Costa Rica, the densely forested birding Mecca of the world, it would be a long list.

Also in this area, we saw plants called "Elephant Ears." We'd seen these before, but along this road they were plentiful. As you can guess from the name, they have huge leaves—up to four feet across. The flowers of these plants heat up at night, wafting out menthol scents that draw in beetle pollinators. A unique adaptation, according to Jonathan.

Jonathan and Manuel were not particularly keen on eating at the lodge, so on the way back we stopped at a little restaurant along the road. We were seated at a long table outside on the patio so we could watch the mountain as we ate. It was too dark to see much, but there were bright little streams of lava running down the mountain and breaking up into red hot clumps that went bounding down the mountainside until they cooled and disappeared. It was also a grandstand seat for the volcano's "whooshes." The dinner was delicious, and we were grateful there were no "ka-booms."

While we ate, Manuel announced that he thought he had the family figured out, so of course we were eager to hear his conclusions. He had Steve figured as Ken's son and Ken, Dorothy, and me as brothers and sister. He pretty well nailed it.

For dessert, Ken and Irene ordered Bananas Flambé. The waiters turned out the lights and brought out a frying pan with bananas in it. They poured in half a bottle of rum and torched it. The rum burned for a while and then, after pouring on more rum, they finally extinguished the fire and served the bananas. Ken licked his plate clean and announced, "Thass the bes' banananas I've never had."

We took his word for it.

Tuesday morning before breakfast, Lorraine and I stepped out on our balcony to gaze at the valley. There were several trees down the hillside. One had ten toucans cavorting around in it. There were also a number of Crested Guans in the same tree and more in an adjacent tree. In the flowering hedge a few feet from our balcony there were several Blue-gray Tanagers, a Kiskadee, a Scarlet-rumped Tanager, and several hummingbirds. All these with the bright morning light on them. A stunning sight!

Cruising down the River

When we finished breakfast in the lodge dining room, we took the bus over to the Peñas Blancas River. There we strapped on life jackets, boarded two rubber rafts, and started drifting down the river. Each raft had a driver, skipper, helmsman, or whatever you call the person steering a raft. Every once in a while Ted and I gave our skipper a hand with the paddling. This was no white-water adventure, just a leisurely float down the river to see what we could see. We saw several troops of monkeys, a few sloths, and a number of birds.

After a couple of hours we paddled to shore and climbed up to a 100-acre homestead/farm. The owner was a ninety-one-year-old, white-haired gentleman who allowed tourists

to stop and visit (for a small fee from the tour company). In return for this income, he had agreed not to cut any more of the forest on his property. We sat on makeshift chairs around several tables under a lean-to attached to the side of his house. It was open on three sides and had a dirt floor. His family served us coffee and cake while we conversed with this old gentleman using Jonathan as an interpreter. He was the grandfather of one of our raft guides.

He was pretty sharp and very interesting. He told me I looked like Eisenhower. I'm assuming that he meant "presidential," and not "bald." He was very astute.

After leaving the perceptive white-haired gentleman we mounted our rafts and floated and paddled down the river another hour or so until we found Manuel hailing us from on top of the river bank. We landed, climbed up the eroding loose-dirt river bank and found Manuel and the bus ready to take us to lunch.

Immigrants

In our discussions with Jonathan about the political situation, we were told about all the Nicaraguans who come across the border looking for jobs and a better, more stable life in Costa Rica. The presence of these people is apparently not always appreciated. Jonathan regaled us with an anecdote:

A Nicaraguan farmer wanted to harvest some timber on his farm. He went to his local hardware store looking for a saw. The manager showed him a chain saw and told him that with this saw he would be able to cut down a hundred trees per day. The farmer took the saw and went home to make his fortune. He worked all the next day but only cut down two trees. The following day he worked every daylight hour and only managed to cut down three more.

He took the saw back and told the store manager it just didn't work. "No sirve," *he said. The store manager looked it over, switched it on, and pulled the cord. The saw let out a roar. It worked perfectly. The Nicaraguan jumped back and yelled, "Ay, what's that noise?"*

The geography may change, but people and their stories don't.

On our float down the river we had seen several groups of bats clinging to the bottoms of tree limbs hanging out over the river. Steve asked Jonathan if they had large bats in Costa Rica. Jonathan said, "No, only about so," holding his hands about eighteen inches apart.

Back to the bus. After a short drive, we stopped for lunch at a resort that had a dining room open to the surrounding gardens. Our table was right next to the edge where we could look out and watch birds and iguanas. Outside in these gardens slices of papaya had been stuck on sticks and hung from the bushes or stuck into the trunks of trees. Many birds were interested in getting their share, including Red-legged Honeycreepers and Scarlet-rumped Tanagers. I shot an inordinate number of pictures at this stop.

After lunch we walked through the resort's arboretum while Jonathan pointed out and told us about all the different trees, shrubs, and plants there. Among many other things, there were cashew and cinnamon trees, along with lemongrass and pineapple plants. We learned that cashew oil is a caustic, phenolic resin that irritates the skin in a manner similar to poison ivy. Needless to say, we just looked.

Butterflies, Beetles, and Sugar Cane

Close by the lodge there's a butterfly garden. Of course we had to stop and look. It's a sizable cage where butterflies are grown—a big family business in Costa Rica. This place was home to a good number of different species, including the big, bright-blue Morpho. I kept trying to get a shot of a butterfly with its wings open, but I never even got close to catching a Morpho in a photogenic position.

As we were getting back into the bus, Jonathan found a Rhino Beetle which was 5½ inches long and 2½ inches wide. It was dead. Alive, it could carry away your Baby Loaf of Tillamook Cheese in one trip.

In Costa Rica they grow sugar cane, and we had seen some earlier in the resort arboretum. Several of our group mentioned they would like to sample some. As we were admiring the huge beetle, Manuel emerged from the arboretum with an armload of sugar cane and his machete. At the next stop he trimmed the cane down to the pulp and put a supply of it in the ice chest for us to chew on. By this time our group's finicky taste buds were off to something else, so the sugar cane didn't get much play. I have to say it's much like chewing on a stick that has been soaked in slightly sweetened water.

When we arrived back at our own lodge, we dropped off Dorothy, Ted, Angie, and Irene, and the rest of us pressed on. We saw a Broad-billed Motmot, a Long-tailed Tyrant, and a Chestnut-mandibled Toucan—fine justification for deserting the others.

We got Steve back in time to meet Angie for their massage appointments at the spa. Steve could never figure why

Angie always got some cute Costa Rican guy to give her massage and he always got Helga, the gal who had passed the physical for the Nazi Storm Troopers. I did notice, however, that Angie was the one who made the reservations.

That evening we went to a different restaurant for dinner as Jonathan and Manuel were still not impressed with the service at our lodge. There was only one other family in the whole dining room. This was one of the rare occasions on the trip when we were free to order whatever we wanted from the menu. The dinner was delicious.

By this time on our trip Steve was learning some Spanish. He was referring to me as "*Mucho Grande* Goofy"—which I'm sure is a high compliment, albeit grammatically incorrect. I try to be a serious-minded influence with this group, but I'm clearly not always successful in that.

In the morning, after some birding, we had breakfast at the lodge again and I tried fried cassava. It has a texture like squash, but is very bland. Definitely not something I'd choose again.

As we left the lodge, Jonathan apologized again for the poor service we had received. None of us had noticed anything except that we'd had to stand in line for breakfast two or three minutes before getting up to the buffet. Oh, and Ken had been unable to get any washcloths.

Man, I can think back to places where we got washcloths but were afraid to use them, where you couldn't stand on the floor of the dining room without your shoes sticking in place, where the sheets had cigarette burns and strange-looking stains, and where the only view was a swimming pool covered with bugs and algae. Nevertheless we all shook our heads and murmured our agreement with Jonathan's assessment, as if we were all scouts for Michelin travel guides.

Shortly after leaving the Arenal area we spied a sloth hanging from an electric wire along the road. It must have been a young one as it almost looked fuzzy and clean. I'm not sure what happened to get him out on that wire, but I imagine his pea-sized brain was working as frantically as a sloth is capable of on ways to get out of his predicament.

We were now on our way to Monteverde on the Pacific side of the Cordillera de Tilarán mountain range. The road runs along the whole northeast side of Lake Arenal—a beautiful drive. We emerged from the mountains into the Guanacaste area of Costa Rica.

The road we traveled was dirt and gravel, full of potholes, and just generally rough and slow. We averaged only about fifteen kilometers per hour. Manuel was all over the road, trying futily to find a smooth surface. There was barely room for two vehicles to pass each other. Manuel had a nerve-wracking habit of using the oncoming lane to escape any unpleasantness in his own lane. As there was much to avoid, we spent a lot of time on the wrong side of the road—even on good paved roads with lines down the middle.

Besides being rough, the road went up, down, around, and back again and again. The countryside was mostly pasture, punctuated with patches of forest. It was dryer than the eastern side of the mountains but still quite green considering we were at the end of the dry season.

During this part of the trip, I passed the gummy worms toward the back of the bus. When they reached Irene and Angie, they just disappeared, as if they had fallen into a black hole. It was the Bermuda Triangle of gummy worms. They did reappear again toward the end of the trip.

Throughout our trip we saw children coming and going from school, loaded down with heavy backpacks and wearing neat, clean uniforms of dark pants/skirts and white tops.

Jonathan often stopped to explain how many peculiarities in what we saw were adaptations to the environment. One plant had ants living inside the hard woody stems. This bush had thorns to protect itself and therefore the ants as well. In return the ants would swarm onto and bite anything that threatened the bush. We saw many similar examples, which made us realize that even we weren't immune to adaptation—for example, Steve's marrying a young set of eyes to keep the group's bird-spotting abilities sharp.

Monteverde

The greater Monteverde area includes the town of Santa Elena with our next home, Monteverde Lodge and Gardens, and the Monteverde Cloud Forest Reserve. Monteverde itself is particularly known for its coffee and cheese.

Let's talk about the cheese first. Every evening our lodge put out a platter of a delicious local cheese with crackers and bread for the guests to nibble on.

Costa Rica grows a lot of coffee. Monteverde coffee is reputed to be world class. We stopped at the tasting room for Café Monteverde, a popular Costa Rican brand, and each couple bought enough bags to take back to all our relatives and friends in the States. The coffee drinkers in our group swore that it was great coffee, with none of the bad qualities of most coffee, i.e.: bad taste, too much acid, bad aftertaste, withdrawal shakes, dizziness, and worse.

I wondered why anyone would bother to drink the stuff in the first place. To me coffee still tastes like soaked ashes from a fireplace. There were also roasted coffee beans for people to munch on—similar to chewing on small pieces of fireplace brick, but without the pleasant texture and flavor. By now you've guessed, I'm not a coffee drinker. My assessment of Costa Rican coffee should be taken with a grain of salt.

The Monteverde Cloud Forest delivered as advertised. Cloud forests occur at mid-to-upper elevations, where mountain ranges intercept the clouds, keeping everything quite wet. They're not *rain* forests, but rather forests that are enveloped in clouds most of the time. The town of Santa Elena sits on the flank of these high hills and is itself rather dry, but just a few hundred meters higher the terrain becomes quite wet.

The Monteverde Lodge was very nice, surrounded by lovely gardens that had the usual paved walkways winding among flower beds, lawns, flowering bushes, and trees. Some trails wound down into a ravine and along a stream. Our room was out on a wing of the lodge where the forests came right up to our windows.

Immediately after lunch, we left to tour another butterfly garden. On the way, Jonathan told us about the scientists who operate it and how dedicated and professional they are. When we arrived, we were assigned a guide who was a kid just passing through Costa Rica working for food and (oh yeah, by the way) to save the rain forest. He was enthusiastic and very much into anything to do with mating, sex, or genitalia.

He started out by showing us a tarantula and letting Ted and me hold it. He also showed us a jar that contained some little beetles crawling around on a piece of bread. He took one out and ate it, explaining to us that people like to garnish salads with them. He then asked if anyone wanted to try one. Only one of us was dumb enough to take him up on his offer. It tasted like mild pepper. The wriggling sure made one want to chew it thoroughly.

Next the young guide escorted us through three butterfly pens. There really wasn't much to see. He carried a long stick to stir up resting butterflies so we could see them better. The whole place was a bit of a disappointment. However, we did get the opportunity to release some newly hatched butterflies into their respective pens. Be still my heart!

At Last, the End of the Family Birding Curse!

When finished with the butterflies, we still had a few minutes of daylight left, so we drove up toward the gate to the Monteverde Cloud Forest Reserve. In the thirty minutes before darkness descended we saw five new birds. We were all hanging around the entrance when Jonathan saw a bird flying over and called out to us, "Come quick! A Resplendent Quetzel!" That got our juices flowing, let me tell you! We searched and searched. Finally Steve spotted it and everyone got a look before it got too dark. Finally the curse on our group was (at least temporarily) broken. We'd had to go to a foreign country to escape it, but the dry spell was over.

Usually on these trips we pick out some rare bird, or even just a common one that most of us haven't seen yet, as our bird-sighting objective for that particular trip. That has usually been the kiss of death—up until now. This was our second time ever actually finding one of our target birds.

This time, we had been bold, some might even say foolhardy, enough to name the Quetzal as our golden standard for the trip. This bird is not easy to see, so we were ecstatic. The Quetzal is bright green on its crested head, shoulders, and down its back. It has black eyes and a yellow beak. It is bright red on its stomach and part way down the tail. The under part of the rest of the tail is white with two or three very long green tail coverts (feathers). These tail feathers are more than twice as long as the body. Altogether this bird is about thirty-nine inches long, not a small thing but rather elusive.

The dinner that night at the lodge was wonderful. I ate way too much. I was working on the theory that with all the activity I could eat whatever I wanted and not gain any weight. I had lost forty pounds in the six months prior to this trip and wasn't anxious to gain any of it back. The theory came close to working. I only gained two pounds. The others scarfed up anything and everything as well without any visible ill effects.

The Cloud Forest

Thursday morning we went back into the reserve and hiked about 2½ kilometers in the cloud forest. We saw a number of birds. It rained just before we started the hike, but only dripped on us while we were on the trails. We were surrounded by dense forest with all kinds and sizes of trees, ferns, vines, and other growing things. Part of the walk took us across a bridge spanning a deep ravine and through the canopy of trees growing up out of the ravine. Some of the medium-sized trees had as many as sixty or seventy species of epiphytes growing on them.

An epiphyte (as it was explained to us) is a flowering plant that clings to a tree and puts out roots that gather nutrients from the mist and from decaying organic matter in the bark of the host tree. These roots creep down the tree toward the ground becoming bigger and bigger, gradually surrounding and encasing the tree. The host tree eventually dies, leaving a hollow area surrounded by all those strangling roots, which remain upright in the shape of the original tree.

It doesn't pay to stand still for too long in these forests.

If the epiphytes are located out on a limb of the parent tree, they also send down dozens of vines—actually roots—directly to the forest floor, searching for soil from which to draw nourishment. These host trees are used by numerous plants in order to either get up to the light or get down to the ground. This whole process can take hundreds of years. It's like a vertical highway system in the forest.

Some of these trees also host up to forty species of orchids, as well as mosses, liverworts, and lichens. In the cloud forest we also saw many "swiss cheese plants." You guessed it—their leaves are full of holes. Their seedlings send out creepers which grow up the tree trunks to get to the light.

Another interesting aspect in all the forests we visited were the massive buttresses sticking out from two to six feet in four or five different directions from the trunks of the trees. They served to give support to very tall trees that had shallow root systems.

Just down the road from the reserve entrance was a place called The Hummingbird Gallery, a gift shop and art studio combination displaying the work of local artists. They also had a small coffee bar and large patio with a number of hummingbird feeders, well-used by numerous species of hummers.

As some of us shopped, others sat outside watching the birds. Ted, who takes about twenty cups per day and can't miss a chance to get in a cup toward his quota, was drinking coffee and noticed a loose board on the coffee bar. He asked the proprietor for a hammer and nails so he could fix it. The guy complied, and Ted did his thing to make Costa Rica safer for all of us. The owner seemed puzzled but appreciative of the gesture.

Quetzals—Even More

A couple of kilometers farther down the road we stopped again. Jonathan and Manuel jumped out and pointed into the forest. Sure enough, they spotted both a male and a female Quetzal. The male was sitting on the nest with the female nearby. After a while they traded posts. The nest was in a large cavity in a tree trunk. The birds were close enough for us to get long sustained views of them.

It was funny to see how excited both Jonathan and Manuel got over a find like this. They were back-slapping and high-fiving, and Manuel gave abrazos all around (remember, Manuel is a big hugger).

We played very cool and ho-hum about the whole thing, but we were pretty excited too. And we weren't at all shy about sharing what we had seen with any other birders we could get to listen to us.

Physical Challenges

We are not a wimpy bunch. But we were doing physical things we weren't used to, in a climate some of us weren't used to, eating more than any of us were used to, and having more time to contemplate aches and pains than we were used to.

As I've mentioned before, we had two doctors, a nurse, and a pharmaceutical sales representative ("drug dealer" might be misunderstood by some) in the group. Both doctors came equipped to handle any and all abnormal bodily functions and real or imagined complaints.

Nearly everyone, it seems, was having neck and/or back problems, nasal problems, hip problems, and sleeping problems. Every time someone mentioned some ailment or dysfunction, several people were Johnny-on-the-spot, trying to hand out some pharmaceutical panacea.

Not wanting my senses chemically dulled, I refrained from any easy solutions, gritted my teeth and toughed it out. No one even offered me anything for my aching teeth.

We returned to the lodge for lunch. A big lunch. Every meal was a major production in quality, quantity, and presentation. Even then, if we weren't given a choice of exotic desserts, some of our group got sort of mutinous. The amount of food we consumed was remarkable. Lunches were not a sandwich-and-chips thing. We always had an entrée, vegetables, salads, rolls, desserts, and one or more fresh fruit drinks along with all the coffee we (or I should say "they") could drink.

Battle of the Frog-Finders

After lunch we waddled back onto the bus and were taken to a place called the Monteverde Frog Pond. It was a tourist trap involving frogs and a pseudoscientific guide to show us around. Jonathan and Manuel were not excited about taking us to this place because they suspected the frogs weren't being treated right. All the frogs on display were endemic to Costa Rica, but they represented only a fraction of the frog species living in the country. Frogs were separated by species into separate terrarium-like enclosures, and one of their gimmicks was to challenge us to "find the frog." These little guys—and a couple really big ones—were well-camouflaged. They can be difficult to find.

Angie revealed a heretofore unknown competitive streak by trying to spot the frog before anyone else could. The rest of us took up the challenge and raced from enclosure to enclosure like little kids, trying to see who could spot the frog first. Lorraine and Angie excelled in this new sport. We got so consumed with spotting frogs that we almost completely ignored the poor guide and his recitations about these imprisoned little amphibians.

Back at the lodge, some of us walked around the gardens looking for—guess what?—birds. The rest of the group relaxed in rocking chairs on the patio. Not that walking around and looking for birds is not relaxing.

Irene's excuse was that she had hurt her knee. Angie's excuse was that she was drawing birds. Ted and Dorothy didn't have an excuse. And they didn't seem to care.

Before dinner Jonathan put on a slide show and gave a short but interesting lecture about the cloud forest.

The Importance of Being Well-Fed

It was at the Monteverde Lodge that Steve first started demanding that peanut butter be served with his breakfasts. The meals we were getting were well-thought-out for balance, nutrition, and presentation, and here he was troweling peanut butter on everything. As if that wasn't enough, Irene asked for and slathered Thousand Island dressing on salads that were already dressed with special chef's creations. It's a wonder they didn't abandon us out in the forest on one of our day trips.

Every time we finished eating, the whole group complained about all the food we were getting fed. Yet by the next mealtime we were all wondering why it was taking so long between courses, even though we had been snacking on bread, cheese, ice cream, soda, and anything else that wasn't nailed down. I've experienced this group when they've run out of food and are convinced that sustenance is being purposely withheld ("withheld" meaning that they haven't eaten for two hours and it's going to be thirty minutes before the next meal). It is not a pretty sight.

I didn't even have to warn the organizers of this trip about this particular peculiarity. They took one look at this group and knew they had better keep plenty of food handy, even though none of us is remotely supersized.

Friday morning we left the Monteverde area and drove south, turning off just before Jacó to drive to Villa Caletas. More about that later. The first hour and a half of this trip we traveled on dirt roads again. Eventually we actually got onto some pavement and made better time. For a while we were driving on the Pan-American Highway.

We saw many "living fences" as we traveled. These are fence posts that have actually taken root and are growing. Some had been trimmed at regular intervals and had grown into trees. We actually saw men out trimming their fence posts.

We stopped for lunch at a small restaurant right on the coast. It was open in front and a nice breeze helped offset the high humidity. With the blue water, palm trees, white-sand beach, and flowering bushes it was a refreshing break from our travel.

After leaving the restaurant, we came to an intersection where there were a dozen or so big rigs parked along the road, farm tractors loaded on their flatbed trailers. We had finally met up with the rice farmers who were preparing to block the road and disrupt traffic to draw attention to their economic plight. Jonathan and Manuel didn't seem to have much sympathy for these guys.

Five Bridges

The countryside was still rather dry, but when we crossed the Tárcoles River, it suddenly changed back to dense, damp forest. Just south of the river we stopped at a trailhead that

Jonathan called Five Bridges. To get there we had to drive a few kilometers up into the hills, where the bus dropped off everyone except Irene and Angie. Manuel was going to take them on to Villa Caletas, where we were staying for the next two nights. As the bus pulled away, rain began to pour down on us. Well, on the bus too, I suppose.

I'd like to report that the bus turned around and came back to see if we wanted to abort our hike—or at least see if we were okay—but that would be stretching the truth. Y'all know how I hate to stretch the truth.

Without a backward glance the bus sped away, leaving us to get soaked and miserable for all they knew. However, a few yards down the trail we found a picnic shelter where we waited for the rain to stop.

Five Bridges trail was exactly what its name implies. The trail weaves its way back down to the main road and in the process crosses five deep ravines on high suspension bridges which put us up in the forest canopy.

Once we left our shelter, the first thing we saw was a long snake. Harmless, but a snake nonetheless. In our group we have a number of highly educated, trained observers. Wouldn't you think we could get a consensus on how long this snake was? We offered estimates ranging from three to eight feet. Since I'm the one writing this, I'll call it five and a half. Not that the length of that snake is going to change anyone's day. It wasn't even poisonous.

As we crossed one of the bridges, several monkeys sat watching us, gradually coming closer and closer, apparently to see if we were real. Suddenly their attention was captured by a squirrel in the treetops. And away they went. It was a great chase and most likely a serious undertaking for the monkeys (as well as the squirrel). The monkeys were hunting for lunch, not just fooling around. The squirrel finally eluded them, but in return, some of the monkeys, out of spite I'm sure, found the squirrel's nest and tore it apart, scattering pieces of it in all directions.

Eventually we met up with the bus on the main highway and rejoined our group.

Villa Caletas

Villa Caletas sits on a high point of land overlooking the *Golfo de Nicoya* to the northwest and the Pacific Ocean to the west and southwest. This is a four-star resort with all the amenities. The driveway from the highway to the Villa was probably four kilometers long, and the views down off both sides of this ridge road were spectacular. We got our room assignments and were led off to locate them along the front of the hillside below the dining areas, patios, swimming pool, and spa.

Lorraine and I found our room down the hillside 118 steps! And it would be another 118 steps to get back up. As I've mentioned before, Lorraine had taken a tumble a few weeks before this trip. She'd fallen down our daughter's stairs, hurting her back, neck, and even her head (which she had wedged against the banister in an attempt to stop her fall). She had been getting sorer by the day, now this! Fortunately, Manuel hauled our luggage for us—both down and back up—or we might be there yet.

Ken, Irene, Ted, and Dorothy had been assigned rooms closer to the top, I'm guessing because of their advanced ages. I suppose Lorraine and I should have been flattered that they thought we could handle all those steps. But by the tenth time coming up them, I would have gladly cashed in that flattery for a room on a higher level.

Our suite was very nice. They had scattered bougainvillea petals around on the bed, on the stack of linens, and on the coffee table in the sitting room. Our balcony doors had a view to the northwest over the forest and the Gulf of Nicoya. We cleaned up some and then climbed all those stairs to watch the sunset from the patio above the dining room. Going down and up those stairs, my knee and hip kept snapping and popping, and Lorraine's ankles were clicking. Together we sounded like the percussion section of a strolling mariachi band.

We didn't finish dinner until around 9:30 p.m., by which time we were all so tired that it's a miracle no one ended face down in the food—which was exceptional, by the way.

At breakfast the next morning, Saturday, among other good things, we had fresh squeezed orange and pineapple juices. They'd probably had someone up since 4:00 a.m. squeezing the fruit just for us. (If you don't appreciate this, just *try* squeezing a pineapple yourself.) But were we appreciative of the effort? Four of our group demanded mango juice instead. See what I mean about getting them back to the rough and tumble of serious bird watching?

After breakfast we went back up to the Tárcoles River to view the crocodiles lying in the river along the banks, just a few feet upstream from the bridge. We weren't the only ones there to see them. There were vendors alongside the road selling all kinds of stuff—carved wooden crocodiles, crosses (the religious ones, not the burn-on-the-lawn kind we have in Texas), stuffed monkeys, other tourist gee-gaws, and several kinds of food. The crocodiles sure enough looked like crocodiles.

Jonathan told us that several months before, one of the managers of the Costa Rican Tourism Board heard that crocodiles were being mistreated in some way, Since they are clearly an asset to the tourist trade, he had traveled from San Jose to check up on them. He had gone down to the riverbank to check on one crocodile in particular that looked poorly and lost an arm in the process of examining it. I don't think Jonathan was kidding.

Before we left, Steve bought some big bean-pod-like

things. Inside the pods were big seeds covered with thick fuzz. We each tried a couple of them, sucking off the sweetish fuzz. We'll probably find out we should have been eating the pods instead of the slow-acting, poisonous, fuzzy seeds. But I guess it wasn't any worse than eating live beetles.

Reserva Biológica Carara

Next we stopped at Reserva Biológica Carara (Carara National Park) and took a hike through the forest. This area was somewhat open, allowing us to see through the trees for some distance. We saw several new birds, including the Royal Flycatcher. Jonathan was really excited about spotting this rather rare bird. Its display involved raising a fan-shaped top-notch. Most fetching if you're a female flycatcher.

Back at the trailhead, we took another trail through a much denser forest. On this trail we heard many birds, but they were hard to spot. Jonathan was good at imitating their calls and was able to draw some of them into open areas where we could get a look. Both hikes were hot and humid, which caused Steve and Angie to talk wistfully about the spa waiting for them back at the Villa.

On one of these trails, I noticed an iguana sitting on a low rock wall. It was gray and black—probably twenty inches long. I put on my long camera lens and took a couple of pictures. Then I walked closer and took another shot. Next I changed to my regular lens and shot another picture. Then I went even closer and repeated the process. All this time I expected the iguana to dash off into the brush. Eventually I stood within a foot of it, and it still sat there enjoying the sun, blissfully uninterested in me.

The Smart Monkeys and the Bees

Back at the trailhead there was a building with some toilets inside and a sink on the outside of one wall. Jonathan suggested that we might want to be careful using the facilities as there was a colony of bees living right next to the sink. This reminded Jonathan of a story his mother had recently told him. She had been watching monkeys playing with a honey-bee nest—their ultimate goal being both the honey inside and the bees, if both could be safely gotten at. They finally solved their problem this way: One of the monkeys chewed up some leaves and made a plug that he stuck into the nest's entrance, effectively sealing in the bees. Then the monkeys took turns easing out the plug. When a bee came crawling out a monkey would pinch it and eat it. When they had finished off the bees, they tore the nest apart and feasted on the honey. Now that's some serious, creative, problem-solving.

Back at the Villa we enjoyed a late lunch, and then everyone went off to do his or her own thing for a few hours. Lorraine tried a siesta to get some relief for her back and neck, while I wrote in my journal.

Later I went to the pool area to sit and write some more. As I ascended the many stairs, I noticed that there was a large iguana walking up the stairs beside me. It was about three feet long and seemed happy to have company on the climb.

Before dinner we all gathered by the pool, talking and laughing. Steve and Angie entertained us by dancing to the wedding reception music coming from the patio next door. They had—how should I say this?—everything in motion with none of it going in the same direction at the same time.

Journey's End

Sunday morning we got up before 4:30, dragged ourselves up the stairs, and boarded the bus. The ride into San Jose was uneventful, except for Dorothy who somehow injured herself and needed first aid, which was rendered by our private, ever-at-the-ready, medical crew.

Along the highway just north of the Villa we saw a tree

with the brightest yellow flowers. It didn't have much in the way of leaves, but it was thick with bright yellow blossoms. Every place we visited in Costa Rica was full of similar flowering trees and bushes. We had stopped to photograph this particular tree the day before, even though there wasn't much in the way of a shoulder to pull off onto. Manuel was very safety conscious, just another thing this group has probably come to expect from their driver in the future. Life can be cruel.

At the airport we said our goodbyes to Jonathan and Manuel and made our way through the international travel maze. Ted and Dorothy got an early flight and left before the rest of us.

It was another wonderful trip, in great company, with lots of laughter and good conversation. Even if we all did get spoiled on this trip, we'll just have to deal with it next year.

The following is a list of the birds that were seen by at least some of the group each day. As a birding reference we were using *A Guide to the Birds of Costa Rica* by F. Gary Stiles and Alexander F. Skutch, which we found to be an indispensable reference book.

Birds we saw on the first day:

Blue-gray Tanager, Great-tailed Grackle, Clay-colored Robin, Rufous-collared Sparrow, Great Kiskadee, Turkey Vulture, Laughing Falcon, Tropical Kingbird, Black Vulture, Broad-winged Hawk, Masked Tityra, Black-cheeked Woodpecker, Groove-billed Ani, Northern Jacana, Variable Seedeater, Purple Gallinule, Scarlet-rumped Tanager, Common Yellowthroat, Blue-black Grassquit, Tropical Pewee, Black-crowned Tityra, Black-cowled Oriole, Ruddy Ground Dove, Rufous Piha, Social Flycatcher, Green-breasted

Mango, Short-billed Pigeon, Scarlet Tanager, Cattle Egret, Golden-hooded Tanager, Black-striped Sparrow, Black Phoebe, Snowy Egret, Mangrove Swallow, Spotted Sandpiper, Little Blue Heron, Black Swift, Anhinga, Olive-backed Euphonia, Bare-throated Tiger-Heron, Ringed Kingfisher, Great Egret, Green-backed Heron, Montezuma Oropendola, Collared Aracari, Purple-throated Fruitcrow, Rufous-tailed Hummingbird, Chestnut-sided Warbler, Slaty-tailed Trogon, and Palm Tanager.

New birds we saw on the second day:

Tennessee Warbler, Long-tailed Hermit, Northern Oriole, Osprey, Common Potoo, Common Black Hawk, Prothonotary Warbler, Sungrebe, Eastern Kingbird, Boat-billed Heron, Scarlet-rumped Cacique, Green-and-rufous Kingfisher, Rufescent Tiger-Heron, Agami Heron (Chestnut-bellied), White-collared Manakin, Barred Woodcreeper, Gray-rumped Swift, White-necked Puffbird, Crane Hawk, Boat-billed Flycatcher, Keel-billed Toucan, Yellow-bellied Elaenia, White-necked Jacobin, Yellow Warbler, Brown Pelican, Band-tailed Pigeon, Common Ground-Dove, Inca Dove, Mealy Parrot, Lesser Ground-Cuckoo, and American Pygmy Kingfisher.

New birds we saw on the third day:

Black-and-white Warbler, White-breasted Wood-Wren, Northern Waterthrush, White-fronted Nunbird, Snowy Cotinga, Boat-tailed Grackle, Hoffmann's Woodpecker, Red-winged Blackbird, Red-billed Pigeon, Red-lored Parrot, Little Hermit, Bronzy Hermit, Crested Guan, Green Honeycreeper, Barred Antshrike, Rose-breasted Grosbeak, Streaked-headed Woodcreeper, Gray Hawk, Black-headed Saltator, Swallow-tailed Kite, Dusky Antbird, Bananaquit, Crimson-collared Tanager, Blue-chested Hummingbird, Purple-crowned Fairy, Scarlet-thighed Dacnis, Common Pauraque, Scaly-breasted Hummingbird, Coppery-headed Emerald, Pale-billed Woodpecker, White-whiskered Puffbird, Ruddy Treerunner, and Black-striped Woodcreeper.

New birds we saw on the fourth day:

Red-legged Honeycreeper, Crimson-fronted Parakeet, Orange-chinned Parakeet, Southern Rough-winged Swallow, Yellow-crowned Euphonia, White-ringed Flycatcher, House Wren, White-crowned Parrot, Barn Swallow, Bronzed Cowbird, Green Kingfisher, Eastern Wood-Pewee, Solitary Sandpiper, Bank Swallow, Roadside Hawk, Buff-rumped Warbler, Common Tody-Flycatcher, Amazon Kingfisher, Rufous Motmot, Squirrel Cuckoo, Long-tailed Woodcreeper, Grayish Saltator, Long-tailed Tyrant, Chestnut-mandibled Toucan, Broad-billed Motmot, Gray-headed Chachalaca, Sulphur-bellied Flycatcher, Slaty Antshrike, Golden-bellied Flycatcher, Great Crested Flycatcher, Dusky-capped Flycatcher, Alder Flycatcher, Slate-headed Tody Flycatcher, and Mountain Elaenia.

New birds we saw on the fifth day:

Brown Jay, Crested Caracara, Great Blue Heron, Olivaceous Cormorant, White-tailed Hawk, White-throated Magpie-Jay, Yellow-faced Grassquit, Eastern Meadowlark, Emerald Toucanet, Steely-vented Hummingbird, Sunbittern, Black Guan, Orange-bellied Trogon, White-throated Robin, Resplendent Quetzal, Violet Sabrewing, Green-crowned Brilliant, Purple-throated Mountain-gem, Blue-crowned Motmot, Striped-breasted Wren, Bay Wren, Black-faced Solitaire, Collared Redstart, and Olive-crowned Yellowthroat.

New birds we saw on the sixth day:

Rufous-and-white Wren, Wood Thrush, Swainson's Thrush, Slate-throated Redstart, Orange-billed Nightingale-Thrush, Gray-breasted Wood-Wren, Red-faced Spinetail, Golden-browed Chlorophonia, Three-striped Warbler, Mountain Robin, Common Bush-Tanager, Yellowish Flycatcher, Ochraceous Wren, Green Violet-ear, Magenta-throated Woodstar, Striped-tailed Hummingbird, White-eared Ground-Sparrow, Gray-crowned Yellowthroat, and Blue-black Grosbeak.

New birds we saw on the seventh day:

Fork-tailed Emerald, Blue-and-white Swallow, White-tipped Dove, Golden-olive Woodpecker, Black-throated Green Warbler, Wilson's Warbler, Rufous-naped Wren, Blue-tailed Hummingbird, Rufous-capped Warbler, Violaceous Trogon, Striped-headed Sparrow, Turquoise-browed Motmot, Laughing Gull, Magnificent Frigatebird, White Ibis, Mississippi Kite, Black-headed Trogon, Black-hooded Antshrike, Spotted-crowned Woodcreeper, Long-tailed Manakin, Buff-throated Woodcreeper, Orange-billed Sparrow, Olive-striped Flycatcher, Scarlet Macaw, Orange-collared Manakin, Dotted-winged Antwren, Buff-throated Foliage-gleaner, Slaty Antwren, and Great Tinamou.

New birds we saw on the eighth day:

Fiery-billed Aracari, Rose-throated Becard, Russet Antshrike, Buff-throated Saltator, Riverside Wren, Greenish Elaenia, Royal Flycatcher, Baird's Trogon, American Redstart, Yellow-throated Euphonia, and Purple Martin.

New birds we saw on the ninth day:

Yellow-headed Caracara, White-winged Dove, Rock Dove, and Blue Grosbeak.

Chapter Six

Desperados Galore

I knew it! It was just as I had prophesied in Costa Rica. This group would never be able to go back to a simple birding expedition after being spoiled by a guided 20-passenger-bus tour with luxury accommodations, someone to handle our luggage, and a guide who found the birds and made sure we saw them.

The moment I saw the size of the luggage coming off the baggage carousels in Tucson, I knew we were no longer the lean, mean birding machine of old. Most of the suitcases were the size of a small pickup truck. It's sad to see loved ones growing soft and lusting after an easy and sumptuous life.

Only Lorraine and I had brought compact carry-on bags. Our sole checked item was a small, blue step stool with a hole drilled in it for our ID tag.

"Step stool?" you ask. Let me explain.

Fifteen-passenger vans are just high enough off the ground to make it a bit of a challenge for some of our group to get in without help. We had bought it on a previous trip just for that purpose.

On this trip we had two new members in the group: Angie's eight-year old daughter Channing and our ten-year old granddaughter Haley. Both had shown an interest in coming on one of these treks, so we decided to expose another generation to the joys, thrills, and educational benefits of birding with the family.

As soon as Lorraine and I picked up the van, we drove the couple of blocks to our hotel, checked in, and found Dorothy and Ted, who had arrived the day before, lounging around the pool. They looked fit and ready to rumble. After a little visit with them, we returned to the airport to pick up Steve, Angie, and Channing.

The Tucson airport is not overly large or complex. There are only two ways most people can get out of the place when they deplane. We took a couple minutes to inhale some Mexican food at the airport restaurant and then planted ourselves right outside the security area they'd be passing through. We waited and waited. The board said their plane had arrived, but they didn't pass our way. They're hard to miss. Steve is well over six feet tall, Angie is very blonde, and there are not many young ladies getting off planes in Tucson with a Kentucky accent as charming as Channing's.

I left Lorraine standing guard at our choke-point and went down to the baggage area. Sure enough, there they were, waiting for their luggage to arrive and wondering where we were. Steve had no idea how they had gotten past us, but he had some story about going through this door and out that door and up some steps and down an escalator. It was all a little vague, but we were glad to see them and soon had them reunited with their massive luggage and loaded in the van for the trip back to the hotel.

After getting them settled and spending a little more time with Ted and Dorothy, we all went back to the airport to pick up Ken, Irene, and Haley. Haley's parents had taken her to Seattle's SeaTac International Airport to meet up with Ken and Irene. Like Ted and Dorothy, they also looked fit and ready to spend four days banging about this part of Arizona looking for birds and enjoying good fellowship.

Right away we learned that Haley didn't have a bathing suit. Since it was in the high 90s and each of our hotels would have a pool, getting her a suit went right to the top of our priorities. Several of us gathered around the hotel's front desk listening to the desk clerk explain how to get to the nearest shops. But once in the van everyone wanted to go off in a different direction. Lucky I was there. They don't call me the "pathfinder" for nothing. Come to think of it, they didn't call me "pathfinder" at all.

Eventually, we found a promising place where Haley could buy a suit while I went into the grocery store next door and picked up some emergency rations to carry in the van, just in case we couldn't find a convenience store or restaurant at some point in our adventure. Remember, I've traveled with these folks before.

I started picking up such essentials as gummy bears, crackers, water, gummy worms, juice, and dried fruit to demonstrate that I did have at least a rudimentary understanding of nutrition. As I stood in the checkout line, I looked over and saw Angie with the two girls, picking up more healthful stuff—such as potato chips. I don't like to dampen people's feelings of empowerment, so I just let them do their own thing. As if I could do anything different anyway.

As we motored around Tucson doing errands, we noticed that the air conditioning in the van just wasn't doing an adequate job. After dropping everyone off at the hotel, Steve and I drove it back to the rental agency. After explaining the inadequacies of their van, we were informed that all the vans were the same way. However, we were driving a Chevy, and they had a Ford sitting right out front. After some more discussion they let us try the Ford, and we found the A/C worked better in that one. We switched vans.

As Steve and I turned into the hotel parking lot we saw a roadrunner. That was the beginning of our bird list for this trip.

San Xavier Mission

Before dinner we took a drive south of Tucson to Mission San Xavier Del Bac, built by Franciscan friars who founded a mission in the area over 300 years ago. It is one of the oldest and most well-preserved missions in the Southwest, famous for its intricately carved altar and the detailed paintings on the interior walls and ceilings—none of which could we see because the place was closed for the day.

Faux Roadrunner

We did begin immediately to see birds—right there in the parking area and around a grotto on the adjacent knoll. At one point Steve grabbed me by the elbow and moved me into position to see a roadrunner beating its prey against a rock in the waning light. It turned out the roadrunner was actually a torn up black garbage bag flapping in the breeze. Even Steve's "young eyes" are apparently not what they used to be.

Haley and Channing dove into bird spotting and watching with as much enthusiasm as they dove into hotel swimming pools. It was obvious that they were the ones with the young eyes, although Angie does quite well too. Come to think about it, Ted and Dorothy still do well at spotting birds as well. As I've said before, it just goes to show what clean living and wholesome thoughts will do.

But First, the Rules...

Before leaving on our first official birding run, I explained to the two new members that the secret to getting the driver to stop the van so they could look at something was to say "Stop." Not "What was that back there"? or "Oh my, that was interesting," or "Why don't you ever stop when I see something interesting?" Haley and Channing didn't seem to have any problem grasping this concept and rather seemed to enjoy yelling "Stop!" and actually have someone obey their commands. Why the older members of the group can't catch on to this simple birding protocol is beyond me.

About the Binoculars

This is a good place to touch on the subject of equipment. Everyone brought their own binoculars, and several of us had more than one pair. Steve had a new pair of 18x50-power image-stabilizing binoculars. With those you can tell the sex of a housefly from a half-mile away. The only problem is that the width of field at any distance at all is about ten feet so you have to know the precise coordinates of that housefly. But once you get your sights on it, he's yours—or she's yours, as the case may be. With these binoculars you can tell the difference.

Haley brought a pair of binoculars that Lorraine and I had gotten her Dad a Christmas or two back. The first day I noticed she was having a little problem finding the birds, so I checked out her glasses. One side worked fine. The other side would not focus at all. When I tipped the glasses up to take a closer look, the fine-focus eyepiece fell off in my hand. The barrel under that eyepiece looked like it had been dropped and dented before someone had tried to glue it back on. They were a lost cause, so Haley used my small glasses from then on. I say "small," but they are 8x40s and worked just fine for her.

In Search of Dinner

Back in Tucson after our visit to San Xavier, we decided to try an Indian casino for dinner. Based on our Wisconsin experience, several of our group were under the impression that casinos turned out excellent fare. Later we couldn't get one person to claim responsibility for that idea. We followed directions to the nearest casino on a series of billboards. It didn't exactly look like it would offer a gourmet dining experience, but Ted, Steve, and I went in and walked around the gaming floor until we found the café, which turned out to be an open place off to one side of the slot machine area, where a person could buy sandwiches, burgers, and such. The cigarette smoke was so thick we couldn't see or smell the food.

Needless to say, we didn't stay to eat.

As I was carefully easing the van into a parking slot back at our hotel, I backed into a cement support for a parking lot light. I just barely tapped the back bumper, but you'd have thought I'd crumpled the back of the van all the way up to the third seat. Everyone jumped out and ran back to survey the damage. They clucked and mumbled, rubbed the bumper where they thought some damage should be, probably taking off more paint than the cement post had. They finally spotted a slight scratch, which with all the rubbing virtually disappeared—so much so that the rental people didn't even notice it when we returned the van a few days later.

Coupons and Time Zones

By the time we were seated in the hotel dining room, we were ready to relax with a cooling drink and turned our attention to the coupons we'd received at check-in. Each room had received coupons for breakfast the next morning and for free cocktails that evening between 5 and 7 p.m., which we had been planning on using during dinner. We checked our watches—yep! We would just make it. But the waiter insisted we were too late. That was a puzzle. Coming from the Central time zone, Lorraine and I had turned our watches back two hours. Those from the Pacific time zone had turned their watches ahead one hour. The Kentucky contingent didn't seem to care one way or the other. This triggered some speculation about what time Tucson was on, or should be on, or thought it was on. We finally figured out that Arizona was one of the two daylight-savings-time holdouts in the country, making everything there happen either before or after you think it should.

None of this had any bearing on anything, but we had missed out on those drinks and didn't want it to happen again.

We did enjoy a good meal while the two young girls swam, watched over by Angie. It was clear that the girls, given half a chance, would rather swim than sit in a restaurant waiting for service. But they *did* allow us to take them some food from time to time.

At dinner we discussed what time to leave in the morning. Some of the more ambitious wanted to be on the road at 7:00 a.m., while others held out for 7:30. We seemed to arrive at a consensus of 7:30, but as we went off to our separate rooms, I wouldn't have bet the price of a candy bar on when we would actually get going.

During the evening, we discussed the increasing frequency of "senior moments," those times when one forgets the simplest things, like where the keys are, or the names of loved ones. Ten minutes later, Steve, age 49, was the one trying to remember the name of a family member. We had thought he'd been talking from observation rather than experience, but maybe not.

An Innovative Way to Reach the Summit

A second topic of spirited discussion involved how Steve was going to make it to the top of 19,000-foot Mt. Kilimanjaro, which he plans to climb in celebration of his

50th birthday. He was concerned about having to carry oxygen, as it might mess up his macho image during photo ops. Someone suggested that maybe the oxygen could be administered via a more unorthodox orifice. We explored this idea at length, concluding that the procedure might revolutionize mountain climbing. Not only would the oxygen be readily available, but by pumping up the volume and mixing in some helium, it could make the climber lighter—thereby reducing the amount of energy needed for the climb. Our only concern was how to get rid of the excess gas after the climb. It would have to be done somewhere private and away from any open flames. Once again, family creative thinking at its finest!

Re-Do the Dew

The next morning we left the hotel at 7:45 and drove all of two miles before we had to stop for some Mountain Dew (Diet of course). You may remember this quest from our trip to the south Texas coast (Chapter Two). Once we got it, we had to have a cooler to put it in and some ice to keep it cold. We finally got back on the road shortly after 8:00.

Gila Monster!

Our first stop was Saguaro National Park. No sooner had we pulled into the visitor center parking lot than a ranger, or someone dressed like a ranger, or at least dressed like we thought a ranger should be dressed, asked us if we wanted to see a Gila monster. Not being a bird, it wasn't on our list of things to see, but how could we possibly pass up such an opportunity? So leaving the van with all the doors hanging open, the whole group went roaring off across the parking lot and out into the desert. By the time we were out of sight of the van I had visions of this "ranger's" friends relieving it of all our valuables. To top it off, only a couple of us actually got to see the Gila monster. When the little reptile went into a crack in a rock wall, the ranger decided to leave it alone, particularly because the wall also housed a rattlesnake. Or so he said.

The Arizona-Sonora Desert Museum

Our next stop was the Arizona-Sonora Desert Museum—a zoo, natural history museum, and botanical garden all rolled into one. We walked the trails looking at everything. Channing and Haley had acquired a map of the place, and were now deciding our route and keeping us on schedule. The museum has an aviary which allowed us to see a number of native birds up close and personal. A docent told us there was a rare bird on the museum grounds which had brought in birders from far and near. We all stood around staring into the treetops looking for a "Blue-throated Orange Nuthatch Oriole," or some such thing. Well, actually what we found was a Yellow Grosbeak—rare in Arizona but in Mexico as common as tequila.

Menominee Firefighters

After the museum we drove down to Buenos Aires, a national wildlife area south of Saguaro National Park. The headquarters compound was only a few miles from the border. We saw more border patrol agents than birds.

As we pulled into the headquarters parking lot, a couple of "Arizona Department of Natural Resources" trucks drove in from another direction. When the drivers got out of their trucks, I asked them if they were doing a prescribed burn in the area. Looking somewhat puzzled, they confirmed that they were. I asked if they had an engine and crew from Menominee Tribal Enterprises helping them. Again they looked puzzled, answering in the affirmative. I handed them a business card. They looked at it and asked, "You're really the President of Menominee Tribal Enterprises?" I answered that I was and would they please tell my engine crew that I stopped by to see how they were doing. They grinned and said they would very much enjoy doing that.

There wasn't much to do around this headquarters area except look at some Masked Bobwhites in a big enclosure, taking part in some kind of bobwhite rehab program.

In this same wildlife area, but over on the east side by the town of Arivaca, we took two hikes—one out across some meadowlands, by a couple of sluggish ponds, and over a boardwalk that crossed some wetlands (at least when they have a wet season). Lorraine had been warned in private by one of the headquarters staff that we should be careful on this boardwalk as there was a rattlesnake that lived under the far end. When Lorraine told us about it we were amused. But I noticed that as we drew near the far end, we just sort of stepped a little lighter. Our second walk ran along a dry river bed through some big cottonwood trees. Everything was pretty dry and dusty. We saw a few birds, but we quickly grew tired, hot, and ready to leave.

Welcome Mr. "Shady"

We found our next hotel in Green Valley. As we all walked into the lobby we saw a nice sign on the counter saying, "Holiday Inn Express welcomes Mr. Steve Shady as our special guest for May 20th." It was a nice sign, in a nice frame, but they had misspelled Steve's last name. It should have said "Mr. Steve Spady." Steve swore he had never been in that establishment before, and that they would have no way of knowing him that well.

For being the day's special guest Steve got a cooler bag with some goodies inside—an easy three-dollar value.

I'll Have That with a Side of Pine Sol, por Favor

Angie found us a good Mexican restaurant for dinner. Good service. Good food. And they put us off in a room by ourselves so we didn't have to worry about disturbing other diners. I'm not sure why we would have worried about that, but it was nice that we didn't have to. The only damper on the evening was that a cleaning lady came in with a mop bucket and, after pouring in a good portion of Pine Sol, filled the bucket with water and started mopping the floor just as they served us dessert. The smell of Pine Sol mixed surprisingly well with the sopaipillas and ice cream. Ted figured they probably soaked their coffee pots in the solution overnight as well. He would be the one to know, as he was the only one drinking their coffee.

Angie's Socks

After dinner we stopped at a dollar store to buy Angie some socks. This was the first of four stops during this trip to buy socks for Angie. I was there and saw it happen and still don't understand it. Socks in Kentucky were a novelty item and hard to come by? On this evening Steve was nominated to go in and buy the socks. He tried the dollar store first.

Now Angie is a lady who designs clothes and, in fact, had just started her own designer clothes company. But for herself she was shopping in a dollar store? It was beyond my comprehension. The dollar store was locked up tight, so I drove over to a nearby Safeway. Steve got out, walked up to the entrance, selected a grocery cart, and pushed it inside. It begged the question: "Angie, what size socks do you wear, anyway?"

Madera Canyon Redux

In the morning we drove up into Madera Canyon, stopping at the Santa Rita Lodge to watch the birds at the feeders. There weren't as many birds as I remembered from our last visit (described in Chapter One), but there were enough to hold our interest for a while. Next we drove up the canyon to the end of the road. From the parking lot there was a sign that said "Nature Trail," pointing down the canyon along the creek. On our last visit, we had taken a rather gentle and rewarding nature trail that followed a meandering creek. So without much more thought, most of us headed down this trail. Ken and Irene somehow smelled a disaster in the making and volunteered to drive the van back down the canyon to the lodge and wait for us there. They even managed to make it sound like they were missing the trail hike to do *us* a big favor.

The trail followed the creek for about fifty yards and then angled up the side of the canyon into the sunlight, the heat, and the dust. We trudged along and along and along. We drew closer and closer to the mouth of the canyon, but we weren't getting any closer to the canyon floor. We discussed going back but then figured that, as long as we were still in the canyon, we couldn't be too lost. Partway along this little stroll some of us, including the two young girls, saw an Elegant Trogon—the high point of the hike.

Nearly three miles later, we switch-backed down the side of the canyon and came out at a parking lot along the road. A three-mile hike was no big deal to any of us, but the psychological difference between what we had been expecting and the reality of the situation was disconcerting. The problem? It was the wrong parking lot. No van. No lodge.

I was convinced the lodge had to be just up the road, so I volunteered to go fetch Ken, Irene, and the transport. When I say "up," by the way, I mean *up*—an extreme gain in altitude. By this time it was very hot in the canyon. Before I left the parking lot, I asked a ranger in a green pickup truck where the lodge was. "About 200 hundred yards up the road," he said. Relieved, I took off.

After about a mile I flagged down two Hispanic fellows in another green pickup. "Is there a lodge up the road?" I asked.

"*Sí, sí,*" they nodded.

"How far?"

"One mile," said one of them.

"One-hundred miles," corrected his partner. Then he changed it to "One-hundred yards."

The entire exchange took place in very broken English.

Encouraged, I trudged on until I came to the end of the road without finding the lodge.

Allowing myself a brief rest to get my heart rate back below triple digits, I headed back down the road. I found Lorraine and Steve eyeing a Flame-colored Tanager just up the road from where I had left them. This was a life-list bird for all of us, meaning this was our first sighting. We walked back down the road together to the trail-head parking area, where Steve volunteered to continue on down to alert Ken and Irene to the fact that they were in the wrong place. Five minutes later the van showed up. The lodge *was* just around the corner. Just *down* the road, not up.

Imaginary Traveling Companions

From the get-go Haley and Channing had staked out the back seat of the van as their territory. A good thing too. No one else in our group could even get back there.

During the course of the trip the girls invented several imaginary traveling companions. One was "Bob." Bob turned out to be some kind of character. At one point he fell face down in a cow pie. Another time he sat on a cactus. Twice Bob got left at stops, much to the relief of everyone. But then he mysteriously showed up again. Bob was so obnoxious a couple of times that several of the other imaginary traveling companions left permanently. Bob had comments to make on a wide variety subjects. I was grateful he kept his feelings about my driving mostly to himself.

After the trials of Madera Canyon, we were hungry. We pulled into a strip mall that advertised a Chinese restaurant, but on our way across the parking lot some of the group spotted a place called Mama's. We stood around the entrance of the Chinese place for a while perusing the menu in the window. Then we all traipsed over to Mama's and had some lunch.

Lorraine and I were hankering for some Southern-style chicken-fried steak, which just isn't available in our part of Wisconsin. Arizona may only be on the fringes of good Southern-style chicken-fried-steak country, but it was as close as we were going to get for a while. And sure enough, Mama had some. It was okay but barely took the edge off our hankerings.

Bellies full, we were ready again to go look for birds.

Back to Patagonia

To get to Patagonia we had to go south through Nogales and then back up to the northeast. Since we were within spitting distance of the border, I suggested to Haley that we cross over into Mexico just so she could say she'd been there. She was quite adamant that Mexico was not on her bucket list.

We had planned three stops in Patagonia. One was the wayside where we had seen a Rose-throated Becard eight years before. Why we thought the Becard would still be hanging around is beyond me, but "twitchers" are funny that way. (WikiPedia defines "twitchers" as "those who travel long distances to see a rare bird that would then be ticked, or checked off, on a list".)

Before we realized it, we had blown by the wayside and were in Patagonia proper. Off we went to site number two—Nature Conservancy's Patagonia-Sonoita Creek Preserve. By the time we got there the place was locked up for the night. Disappointed, we went back to town and tried the backyard of the Patons, who you'll remember from Chapter One. We were graciously invited in to stay a while and see the birds. In addition to chairs, benches, and awnings, they had hung out four hummingbird feeders, as well as some other types of feeders, but the activity was not nearly as frantic as it had been on our previous visit, although we did see several different kinds of hummingbirds.

Our hosts also told us where to go back along the preserve road to see a Zone-tailed Hawk's nest. You can imagine our excitement. *And* if we continued past that and cut over to the highway, we would come out near the wayside where we should be able to see that Rose-throated Becard. We found the hawk's nest and spotted several of its feathers sticking out over the edge of the nest. Then it was on to the wayside where we spent a few minutes half-heartedly looking for the Becard before moving on—not the kind of intensity one might expect from an avid group of birders, but it was getting late.

A Threat to Security

We left Patagonia in the rear-view mirror, heading for Sierra Vista and our hotel. On the way, as we traveled through very open, rolling, semi-arid countryside, we came up behind a strange vehicular configuration. The central player in this convoy was a wide load of something we could not identify from our distance. It was desert tan, which we thought quite sinister. There were two police cars in front directing oncoming traffic onto the shoulder to assure its safe passage. There was another police car following, with three army vehicles bringing up the rear. Our group decided that, at the very least, the wide load was nuclear material of some sort, probably waste or maybe even warheads. After all, if a terrorist organization wanted to bring in some weapons of mass destruction, what better way than to make it look like real police and army escorts were involved? We kept our distance to avoid getting irradiated or caught up in a terrorist plot.

Suddenly, one of the army vehicles had a flat tire. All three of them pulled off the road. We were certain the tire had been shot out by whoever didn't want this shipment to reach its destination. Or perhaps someone was trying to hijack the sinister load. You can see we had quite a scenario going at this point.

We drove around the sidelined army contingent and pulled up behind the state patrol vehicle in an attempt to assure him that he needn't worry now that we were covering his six.

The closer we got, the more the wide load looked like a big ordinary piece of industrial machinery. Irene pointed out that this was exactly the kind of cover an evil genius would pick to disguise his true purpose.

Very shortly after this we drove into a small community at a crossroads, and the convoy pulled off to the side of the road. We eased past and continued on our way. The nuclear load indeed turned out to be nothing more than a big industrial machine, and the police cars were merely police cars.

Considering the speculation that had consumed us for the previous twenty miles, it was amazing how quickly the whole subject was dropped. Some of us have clearly been watching way too much television!

The Two Canyons of the Santa Rita Mountains

The hotel in Sierra Vista turned out to be very nice. We got directions to a couple restaurants from one of the most helpful clerks I'd encountered for a long time. After a few minutes to clean up, we chose the closest establishment and went to get something to eat. It billed itself as a steak house and looked pretty good. As soon as Steve realized I was going to pay for the meal, he ordered *two* steaks.

During the meal we talked about a family reunion—an idea that several of the nephews and nieces have espoused, although to date no one had volunteered to carry the ball. We decided that it was high time to move on the idea. But as we talked and no one stepped forward to take command, Steve and I finally agreed that we would work on it. In two minutes we had decided the when and the where. Ken and Dorothy, nervous at what they perceived as our autocratic approach, decided that their more sensitive and democratic natures might be better suited to contacting everyone and setting up the arrangements. Steve and I sullenly—or at least we hoped it looked that way—acquiesced.

The next day we picked two canyons to explore. Both reach up into the eastern flanks of the Santa Rita Mountains. Angie and the girls opted to stay in town to swim and hang out.

First we visited the world-famous Ramsey Canyon Preserve. Because we had been here before, we were familiar with its attractions. We hiked up the road which follows the floor of the canyon alongside a creek, where we saw a number of birds. When we got back down to the preserve headquarters/gift shop, there was a tour guide expounding to his group about what they would see in the canyon. While we hung around listening to this gentleman, who seemed to really know his flora and fauna, a turkey strolled around us. The tour guide identified it as a Mexican Wild Turkey. We witnessed a moment of drama when suddenly a fox dashed out of the rocks and chased the turkey up into a tree.

Next we moved on to Upper Miller Canyon, which was higher in altitude than Ramsey Canyon—up around the 7,000-foot mark. While walking around here, we ran into the owner/caretaker of a bed and breakfast located in the mouth of the canyon. According to him, we would find Red-faced Warblers and Spotted Owls up the canyon trail. We all wanted to see them, so we asked for more details.

The caretaker used the tip of the handle of his garden rake to draw a map in the gravel. Although there was only one trail, he managed to make it sound quite complicated. One-third of the way up the trail, he explained, we would find a landmark called "Split Rock." Two-thirds of the way up was "The Telephone Booth." He assured us that both landmarks would be hard to miss. The Spotted Owls, he said, were about three miles up the trail. He kept using the word *up*, which none of us thought to question at the time.

This caretaker also told us about a nice resting place, just off the trail a couple hundred yards from the trailhead, that could be used by those who might not want to go to the top. I couldn't understand why he seemed to aim this at me.

By the time he was done, his drawing in the gravel looked as if someone had spilled a bucket of worms, each one headed in a different direction. Finally he mentioned that to get to the trail, we had to pass through two locked gates. He gave us the combinations to both. He made it sound like a favor when he said that there was normally a charge for being allowed to take this shortcut to the canyon trail. In retrospect, I'm convinced he made up for this lack of revenue with income derived from renting out defibrillator paddles, nitro tablets, and pulls on his oxygen bottles.

Lorraine once again mentioned that she had never seen a Spotted Owl. I reminded her about the "Logging & Spotted Owl Symposium/Barbecue" we had attended in Spokane back in 1986. She admitted that she remembered, but she thought they might look different with their feathers on. Of course we were just kidding. Where could you possibly find a Northwest logger who would barbeque a Spotted Owl?

Flirting with Heart Failure

Naïvely, we started up the road, which soon turned into a steep trail with the surface of a rocky creek bed. When I say "steep," I mean it was like a three-mile shallow set of stairs with very poor footing. (Remember we were already at 7,000 feet in elevation.) What with the burning leg muscles and the wheezing and the gasping, I had no idea how the others were doing. I had to hold one hand over my mouth just to keep from sucking up trail debris. I finished the climb with a sore tongue—from stepping on it all the way up the trail.

At one point, a couple of other guys came strolling past

us and Steve asked if they had seen any Red-faced Warblers. "You mean like that one over there?" asked one of them. Sure enough, there sat one of the little red-faced birds, not more than fifteen feet away. These two hikers stuck close for the rest of the way up the trail. I suspected they were looking forward to a chance to practice their CPR.

Steve made the hike okay. Ken made the hike okay. Ted and Dorothy made the hike okay. Lorraine made the hike okay. I was the only one who had gasped and wheezed the whole way. And Irene? She'd had the good sense to stay in the van the whole time, in the shade, sucking on cold water and gummy worms.

On our way up this hellish canyon trail we encountered a string of Hispanic men headed in the opposite direction, each toting a small nondescript pack. It seemed clear they were not up in those mountains looking for birds. The only thing behind them was the border. When they spotted us, they came to a dead stop, looked us over a moment, and then moved on, evidently deciding we didn't look like "la migra." The fact that one of us looked rather green and didn't seem to be able to breathe probably assuaged their fears.

For lunch we caught up with Angie, Haley, and Channing in the food court of the Sierra Vista Mall. After our exertions of the morning, any food would have tasted great. Not that it was bad, but the exercise certainly seemed to enhance its quality.

San Pedro River

After lunch a couple of our group volunteered to stay near the pool with the young ladies while the rest of us drove about seven miles east of town to the San Pedro Riparian National Conservation Area. This 36-mile-long stretch of cottonwood trees and brush along the San Pedro River is like a green oasis cutting through this part of the arid Arizona landscape. It was the first area in the United States designated as a Globally

Important Bird Area. When we got to San Pedro House (the headquarters building), we watched a woman banding hummingbirds. It was very interesting to see how delicately she handled, inspected, and weighed these fragile creatures.

We considered taking one of the trails along the river, but because it was coming up on dinnertime we headed back to the hotel. Prompt feedings nearly always trump birds with us.

On the way back into town we happened upon the Sierra Vista wastewater wetlands, where locals have built a bird-watching station overlooking the settlement ponds. We saw a number of birds there.

In the morning we loaded up all our stuff and took Highway 90 east. After a short stop at the wastewater wetlands again, we went back to the San Pedro Riparian area. We walked a trail which took us out along the river for a ways, around a couple of ponds, and back to the parking lot.

A Medical Emergency

Near one of the ponds we encountered numerous large potholes in the trail, ranging from 12 to 36 inches across and just as deep. As we were concentrating on one particular bird, Lorraine took a step back and fell into one of the bigger holes. Ken and I each quickly grabbed her arms and lifted her out, but the fall had taken the skin off one of her knuckles, the heel of the same hand, and her elbow. People gathered around to help assess the damage. Someone offered some tissue to help clean off the dirt and blood that was starting to ooze out of her wounds. Haley gave comfort by patting Grandma on the back and putting her arm around her, assuring her everything would be okay. With limited first aid equipment on hand, the best we could offer was a clean handkerchief. Our medical crew was surprisingly under-equipped this time out.

Back in the van we set our sights on Tombstone. Being the unerring pilot that I am, that's right where we ended up.

Just prior to getting into Tombstone, Lorraine's camera came apart. The latch for the door over the film cavity broke off, and that was the end of her picture-taking. This particular camera had survived more trips in Lorraine's hands than most. The vast majority of them have succumbed to being dropped, soaked in salt water, stepped on, thrown around, or just generally molested in some fashion.

Tombstone certainly didn't qualify as hardcore birding, but it was our last day, and we felt some variety in our itinerary might be in order.

Desperados Galore

We pulled into town, parked the van a block off Main Street, and started out to see what we could see.

Tombstone got its start in the late 1800s when a prospector found a bunch of silver ore in the nearby hills. In its heyday it was the biggest town between St. Louis and San Francisco. Of course, Tombstone is best-known for the gunfight between the Earps and the Clantons at the OK Corral. The participants included Wyatt Earp, Doc Holiday, a couple of Wyatt's brothers. The Clantons and the Lowry brothers didn't survive the festivities.

On Main Street the locals were getting ready to do one of their gunfight skits, so we hung around the boardwalk and watched. There were desperados galore. One of the tough-looking characters strolled over to talk with Haley and Channing. The girls weren't so sure if they wanted anything to do with this mean-looking *hombre*. These staged gunfights are performed 365 days a year in Tombstone. In addition to the skits there are stagecoach and wagon rides up and down Main Street all day.

Afterwards we ducked into Big Nose Kate's Saloon for some lunch. This saloon had once been the hangout of Doc Holiday, who was sweet on Kate.

There was a bar along one wall, while tables filled the rest of the restaurant. On the other wall was a small bandstand where a DJ/singer/keyboard player was performing. We took the two tables right next to the singer, got menus, and ordered. Steve, Lorraine, and I had the buffalo burger, which was very tasty.

At one point Ken stood up and stepped away from his table to take a couple of pictures. "You a professional photographer?" the DJ/singer asked him. Thanks to his microphone the whole saloon heard him.

"No," replied Ken.

"You a pimp?"

"Nope."

"Well, you have that look," came the response.

The crowd seemed to find this uproariously funny.

Later the DJ/singer started the following routine: When someone new entered the saloon he would ask where they were from. They would name a state or town like "Maryland."

"Maryland?" he would exclaim incredulously.

Then the whole restaurant would shout, "No sh-t!"

The reactions from the targets of this exchange were varied. Some laughed and some beat a hasty retreat. This appeared to be the height of entertainment in Tombstone.

During part of his act, the DJ/singer picked up a feather boa, came down from his platform, wandered around a little, and then came over and wrapped the boa around Haley's neck, putting his head down by hers so we could take a picture. He then went and got a black hat for Channing. The girls loved it. Haley kept the boa on the whole time we were there. Soon after leaving, Angie slipped off with the girls and bought them each a feather boa. The rest of the trip, the only time Haley was without hers was when she was in the water.

After lunch we moved down the street to one of those old-time photo parlors where you can dress up in period clothes for a tintype-style photo. We picked the "WANTED DEAD OR ALIVE, REWARD $25,000 IN GOLD COIN will be paid by the U.S. Government for the apprehension of

THE WILD BUNCH" pose. Each of us chose the character we wanted to be. Ken was Wyatt Earp and I was one of the Earp brothers. The photographer busily snatched outfits off the racks, helping everyone into their costumes. If an outfit was too big, she clipped the back with alligator clips to take up the slack. We looked pretty tough until you saw us from the back. It's pretty hard to take Wyatt Earp seriously when he's got alligator clips holding his clothes on.

Once we were all costumed, we selected our hats, gun belts, and firearms. Then we were posed up against a bar while the photographer took several different shots. We picked the one we liked best, and she started cranking out prints for everyone. A more desperate-looking gang of desperados hadn't been seen in Tombstone before or since.

Angie observed that Ken looked like Wyatt Earp on a really bad day. I thought she was being kind.

And the ladies! I certainly understand the old Indian fighter's prayer: "God, please don't let me fall into the hands of the squaws." Even Haley and Channing. Who would have imagined they could look so tough? We exited the shop in stitches.

By this time Lorraine's arm was really starting to hurt. The two of us headed into a drug store down the street and showed the clerk the arm. She went right to work sweeping stuff off the shelves as she told us what she intended to do. Happily it turned out she was a nurse. Not only did she gather up what we needed, but she put some paper towels on the counter and proceeded to patch up the arm. Peroxide, cleanup, antibacterial salve, gauze pads, tape, elastic wrap—she had everything we needed. The whole operation, including materials, cost us $9.00 and change. It was an impressive performance.

While we were getting first aid, the rest of the group went over to watch the Shoot-Out at the OK Corral. Lorraine and I got there late but in plenty of time to witness the carnage.

After doing as much as we felt we needed to do in Tombstone, we took off for Tucson, but not without a stop for snacks. After all it *had* been several hours since our last meal at Big Nose Kate's.

The Last Night

Back in Tucson nearly everyone went swimming. I redeemed two of our free-drink coupons and got Lorraine and me each a virgin margarita. I let Haley try mine just to prove how bad the thing really tasted. She wasn't disappointed.

Later we had dinner on the terrace between the hotel and the pool. While we ate, we discussed where to go next year. It seemed to boil down to one of two destinations—Alaska or Belize.

Part of our dinner entertainment was provided by Channing and Haley regaling us with one "blonde" joke after another. Channing, especially, can go on all day and never repeat herself. She's a born storyteller.

Jinxed Again!

If you haven't yet noticed, we've not listed a Painted Bunting as one of the birds observed. As usual, we had jinxed the sighting of this poor bird by naming it the "must see" bird of the trip. All the literature said they were available in almost epidemic proportions in a number of the places we had visited. But did we see one? Nope. After our success in Costa Rica, the family curse was back.

The Clan Heads East

The Kentucky and West Virginia contingents took the hotel shuttle to the airport early the next morning. Lorraine and I took Ken, Irene, and Haley to the airport in the van, said our goodbyes, returned the van to the rental place, and caught our flight to Green Bay.

It was a great trip. We even managed, among all our other hijinks, to see quite a few birds. Having the two young girls along was an added bonus this year. They did their part in spotting birds and Haley lugged her heavy bird book wherever we took ours. But, as always, birding is only part of why we take these trips. The fellowship, laughter, and just catching up is the best reason of all.

Birds we saw on the first day:

Greater Roadrunner, Gambel's Quail, Pyrrhuloxia, Cactus Wren, House Sparrow, Curve-billed Thrasher, Gila Woodpecker, and Mourning Dove.

New birds we saw on the second day:

Canyon Wren, Common Raven, Verdin, Turkey Vulture, Yellow Grosbeak, Canyon Towhee, Red-tailed Hawk, Harris's Hawk, Barn Swallow, White-crowned Sparrow, Masked Bobwhite, Blue Grosbeak, Vermilion Flycatcher, Black Phoebe, Summer Tanager, Phainopepla, Red-winged Blackbird, Western Kingbird, Black-bellied Whistling Duck, Great Blue Heron, Gray Hawk, and Say's Phoebe.

New birds we saw on the third day:

Western Scrub Jay, Gray-breasted Jay, Purple Finch, Acorn Woodpecker, Strickland's Woodpecker, Black-headed Grosbeak, Broad-billed Hummingbird, White-breasted Nuthatch, Brown-headed Cowbird, Lesser Goldfinch, Black-chinned Hummingbird, Blue-throated Hummingbird, Elegant Trogon, Black-throated Gray Warbler, Flame-colored Tanager, Bridled Titmouse, Double-crested Cormorant, Black Hawk,

Lazuli Bunting, American Coot, Cassin's Kingbird, Zone-tailed Hawk, Thick-billed Kingbird, White-winged Dove, and Violet-crowned Hummingbird.

New birds we saw on the fourth day:

Mexican Wild Turkey (Gould's), Painted Redstart, Hepatic Tanager, American Robin, Western Wood-Pewee, Magnificent Hummingbird, Sulphur-bellied Flycatcher, Western Tanager, Rock Wren, Red-faced Warbler, Brown Creeper, Great-tailed Grackle, Ruddy Duck, Snowy Egret, Black Duck, and Killdeer.

New birds we saw on the fifth day:

Northern Mockingbird, Rock Dove, Mallard, Redhead, Black-necked Stilt, Anna's Hummingbird, Albert's Towhee, Yellow Warbler, White-fronted Swift, Common Yellowthroat, and Yellow-breasted Chat.

Chapter Seven

Georgia on My Mind

I know you've all been holding your breath since the last birding trip to find out if we were ever able to spot what had been our must-see bird for the last three trips in the U. S.—the Painted Bunting. Actually it's not uncommon in many locales in the U.S., but it's certainly been elusive enough to avoid being seen by us. (There are some who would say that doesn't take much.) There's been talk of a jinx all along the way; but no one could prove it was my fault, so once again the Painted Bunting was the bird to see. And did we? Read on.

Gathering the Gang

The day before our trip, Lorraine and I went over to Enterprise car rental in Lexington, Kentucky, and picked up our mini-bus, also known as a 15-passenger van. The next morning, after loading in a few clothes, water, soft drinks, and snacks, we left Lexington at 5:45 and drove south. We picked up Steve at a Chevron station along the freeway in London. He seemed bright-eyed, bushy-tailed, and ready for the trip, although he was pessimistic about our chances of seeing much, as all the birds he'd seen migrating north past his place had Georgia plates. We hoped there would be a few left down south.

In Atlanta we found Ken and Irene, along with Ted and Dorothy, waiting for us at the Airport Marriott. We were glad to see Ken up and around and using both arms. A couple days before leaving for Atlanta, Ken had tried an innovative method of descending a flight of stairs, finishing off his acrobatics on his left shoulder. His first thought while trying to take inventory of all his limbs: "I wonder if I'll be able to hold up a pair of binoculars?" What a guy! He did fine, except for avoiding any heavy lifting or much contact with that left shoulder. We never did hear what pain medications he was self-prescribing, but whatever it was, it didn't seem to affect his performance. Ted and Dorothy looked their same spry selves.

Special Accommodations

We did have several other medical concerns—Irene's knee and Lorraine's back and leg. We had all decided that they would have to do only what they could and promised not to worry about what they couldn't.

Steve had called two days before we left to suggest that we needed something more substantial than the simple little step stool we'd used for the past few years to help certain folks get into the van. Lorraine and I ran all over Lexington calling on medical supply houses trying to find something that would work. One intriguing item is an easy chair that tips up and sort of catapults the passenger through the van door. Finding exactly the correct setting might have been a challenge, but I'm sure it would have taken only a dozen or so experiments to figure it out. We finally settled for a stool that has a handrail attached to one side. The nice thing about it is that the last person in can just reach out, grab the handle, and pull it up into the van. Steve also had some questions about Depends and Porta Potties, but we felt confident he would be okay without either.

Benevolent Dictator

Our destination was Waycross, Georgia. We loaded the van and established our seating arrangements: Lorraine and I up front, Ken and Ted in the next row, Dorothy and Irene in the third row, and Steve way back in the fourth row by himself. The reason I mention this is that it was not always easy to hear Steve speaking from that far back. Between Atlanta and Waycross, Steve told several jokes. There was one about three boys in the third grade having some kind of contest..., ending up with "but son, you're 23 years old!" There was something in the middle that apparently made this very funny, but like I said, I didn't catch everything that came from that fourth seat. It was probably just as well.

It had been raining all the way down from London, but between Atlanta and Waycross we had some real toad-choking downpours. (I got that expression from Chip, whom you'll meet later.) The rain nearly brought traffic to a standstill—down to at least forty or fifty miles per hour. But we just kept plugging along and soon found our motel in Waycross. The main reason for Waycross was its proximity to Okefenokee National Wildlife Refuge, our destination for the next day.

Once we got settled in Waycross, the eternal question was raised, "Where should we eat?" This discussion gave rise to the term "benevolent dictator," a phrase that was used and discussed numerous times over the next few days, not only in the context of picking an eating establishment, but in connection with national and world politics. At one point Ted actually volunteered to take on the job here in the U.S.

Finding Fine Dining in Waycross

We hadn't found a wide variety of choices for eating out in Waycross. At Applebee's we all had our hunger satisfied with reasonably tasty and tastefully presented food.

Before we ordered our meals, the waitress took our drink orders. Some of us merely asked for water. Dorothy requested lemonade, and Ted had his coffee. Steve demanded something with alcohol in it. (The rumor that this had something to do with my driving was greatly exaggerated.) Before the waitress would take his order for a Bombay Sizzle Fizz Smoothie, or whatever it was he had ordered, she demanded to see his driver's license. Steve was closing on 52 years of age at a pretty good clip at the time, so I think the waitress was just trying to be cute.

When traveling like this, each couple pays for their own food, just to cut down on wrangling like "It's your turn to pick up the tab, I got it last night" or "But last night we were eating at McDonalds and now we're here at Chez François." Each time, before telling the waiter what we wanted, one of our group would explain that we needed separate checks—"One for those two, one for those two, one for those two, and one for this guy who's by himself." Toward the end of the meal, the waiter referred to the split checks as "water/water," "coffee/lemonade," "decaf/water," and in a sad voice, "single." It sounded so pitiful. (Angie, are you paying attention? Angie is Steve's wife who lucked ou . . . er, I mean couldn't join us on this trip.)

Before returning to the motel, we went down to the north entrance of the Okefenokee swamp to see what we could see. Because it was nearly dark and the entrance was shut, we didn't see much.

"The Swamp"

Okefenokee is 700 square miles or 438,000 acres of freshwater wetlands—locals affectionately call it "The Swamp." It reaches nearly all the way from Waycross, Georgia, 38 miles down to the Georgia-Florida border. It is about 25 miles wide from east to west. There are several entrances to the refuge, and Thursday morning found us up with the

sun and driving down to the east entrance to the Suwanee Canal Recreation Area, the main Fish and Wildlife entrance. We had reservations with an outfit appropriately named Okefenokee Adventures for an all-day boat trip out into the Swamp. We got signed in and filled out our menus for lunch (which brought on the first crisis of the day—they had no pastrami for Ted). Then we piled into a boat and started out.

Our boat driver and guide was Chip, half owner of the business. His wife was the other half. She ran the rest of the staff, took care of the gift shop, and kept up the insurance—we hoped.

Chip knew more about the Swamp than any one person ought. We expected to see it teeming with wildlife, but all we saw was the occasional bird or alligator and not much else. Chip's explanation? "All the herons must be at the rookery. The 'gators are all spread out. The 'gators have just finished breeding and are too tired to lay in the sun. I saw a bittern right there once. See that speck in the sky?—it's an Anhinga. My wife saw a Red-cockaded Woodpecker here last week. And hear that? That's a Pileated Woodpecker." But could we find it? No! Chip continued filling in the gaps with a continuous narrative about the Swamp, its history, its ecology, and numerous other interesting facts and figures.

Even without the wildlife, the swamp water was black and the reflections of the surrounding trees and other flora were spectacular.

Let me throw in here that what with the hanging Spanish moss, "land" that seems to move of its own accord, swamp gas bubbling to the surface, and all the curious creatures that call this swamp home, the place can be a little spooky, especially at night. Sightings have been reported of UFOs, Bigfoot, and even some *really* far-out things. We were glad to be doing this trip in daylight.

Our boat was a flat-bottomed skiff with a single outboard motor to push us around and a canopy to keep off the sun. It could carry up to fifteen people, so the seven of us were able to spread out very comfortably.

We motored out the old Suwannee Canal to get into the Swamp and then followed waterways which wound through the prairie connecting the ponds and small lakes. The Swamp has over 120 miles of paddle- and motorboat trails—plenty of places for interested nature lovers to roam. These trails were often not much wider than the skiff.

In the shallow waters (which nearly all of it is), the water lilies rooted on the bottom create a thick mass of roots, which decompose, creating methane. Big globs of this matter rise to the surface. Grasses, palmetto, and small trees sprout on these globs, forming floating islands that can't be told from solid ground unless you try to walk on them. It's a bit like walking on a waterbed. The early native people, not having a word for waterbed, called the place Okefenokee, or Trembling Earth. A couple of times we had to push these floating islands out of our way in order to proceed.

Around noon, after crossing a small lake, we pulled into one of the camping platforms that dot the Swamp and had some lunch. With enough of a breeze to keep the bugs at bay, it was very pleasant. Chip had a large repertoire of interesting swamp sayings, one of which was that "toad-choking rain" I referred to earlier.

After the boat trip, we took the nine-mile scenic loop on Swamp Island Drive, a self-guided tour through different habitats with wildlife clearings, wetlands, and hardwood plots. As we started out, Ken declared he was going to keep his eyes peeled. We all appreciated his excruciating sacrifice.

This area is where we hit birding pay dirt. We saw a Red-cockaded Woodpecker and a Pileated Woodpecker. Both of these were firsts for some of us. Someone had painted white rings around the trees where the Red-cockaded Woodpeckers were nesting, which helped us find them. Out at the end of the drive there was a trail to a tower which we climbed. It gave us a bird's-eye view out over many acres of swamp. With our binoculars we scanned every inch of the vista, only spotting two ducks and an alligator.

For a little while there Dorothy and I thought we had discovered some strange and unique bird preening itself on the water's surface. Then Steve come along with his 40-power stabilized binoculars to tell us it was a lily pad being kicked up by the wind. Speaking of Steve's binoculars, he could clearly see all the way over to Alabama, while the rest of us were struggling to see things a mere fifty feet from the ends of our noses.

When it got too dark to see much of anything, we drove back up to Waycross and our motel.

Contrary to the prognostications of the weathermen, the weather had been great. The thunderstorms they had predicted never came to pass.

That evening, after considerable debate (during which that pesky subject of the benevolent dictator came up again), we settled on Ruby Tuesday for dinner. Dorothy and Ken had been looking forward to a Ruby Tuesday veggie burger all day. When the burgers arrived, Dorothy swore that the patties were made of ground-up carrots and some other mutilated vegetables mixed with a large quantity of swamp fiber. Other than her disappointment, the food was okay, and the salad bar was excellent. We got out of there around 9:40 p.m.

Luckily, we didn't have to get up "with the birds" the next morning, even though ostensibly that was the whole reason for our trip. We had breakfast from the serve-yourself breakfast bar at the hotel and then packed the van and drove southeast to the coast just a few miles above the Florida border.

Birding the Georgia Coast

We started the day at Crooked River State Park—five-hundred beautiful acres on Georgia's coast. The park is located about seven miles north of St. Marys. The portion of the park we spent time in was right up against the Atlantic Intracoastal Waterway. All the places we stopped to bird are on Georgia's Colonial Coast Birding Trail.

Georgia seems to be a latecomer in realizing there is a lot of money to be sucked out of birders. Only recently have they banged together some birding trail maps and literature, listing all the places where the locals have seen a bird. Some of their choices were good and some were rather a mystery.

This state park was an okay place. We walked a couple trails and did see some birds, but naturally we were about two weeks early for the Painted Buntings. We stopped at the visitor center to file a complaint, and the employee there was kind enough to call Skidaway Island State Park to see if they had any Painted Buntings there. Sure enough, some were using their feeders, and they promised to hold on to them until we could get there.

As we exited the state park, the group made it plain that I had about ten minutes to find them a place to eat—or else! They were desperate. They obviously didn't consider the duffle bag full of crackers, cookies, gummy worms, gummy bears, and power bars, along with cases of spring water and Mountain Dew, sufficient for their short-term needs. Never mind the snack standards to which their palates had become accustomed in Costa Rica. Just in time I found a Kitchen Basket—no, a Breakfast Barrel—no, try *Cracker Barrel* restaurant. We got everyone fed in the nick of time and back on the road.

All along the Georgia coast there are numerous offshore, barrier islands. Some of these are connected to the mainland by causeways, and a few of these causeways have roads on them. Our next stop was Jekyll Island. There were supposed to be birds on the causeway, as well as on the southern and northern ends of the island. The list of birds that had been seen in this vicinity was impressive and exciting. But all we found were a couple of pelicans and a few seagulls. The literature explained that most of the listed birds could be best seen at high tide. Guess where the tide was when we got there?

Our next stop was St. Simons Island at the end of another causeway. According to the literature, it should have been covered with birds, including the elusive Painted Bunting. Once again we found the advertising to be on the verge of criminally misleading.

Most of these islands look to be about two feet above sea level and are covered with houses, or in the last two cases, small towns. We wondered what they did during hurricane season, besides talk to their insurance agents.

Evening found us checking into an Embassy Suites in Brunswick, Georgia. I knew this place had an address on Mall Boulevard, but we were a little surprised to find that this hotel was actually *part* of the Mall.

On this trip Irene had brought along her handicap parking permit to put in our windshield so we could officially take advantage of handicap parking spaces. We quickly grew accustomed to this parking advantage. Everyone would start looking for the handicapped parking signs the moment we pulled into any parking lot. It was a legitimate blessing, as two of our members found it very painful to do much walking.

We checked into our rooms and went down to the lobby for free drinks and snacks—part of the "Welcome Home" policy of the Embassy Suites. Once again the problem of where to eat arose, and once again we beat the subject to death. We had a choice of driving someplace or eating at the Ruby Tuesday right there in the Mall. Nobody was much inclined to get back in the van, so we opted for Ruby Tuesday again.

Big mistake!

The satisfactory experience of the night before had lulled us into a false sense of security. Several of us went for the salad bar, since the one the night before had been excellent. Well, this one was terrible—stuff slopped all over the place, half the bins empty, and the whole thing just grubby-looking. We struggled through, getting just enough to keep us alive until breakfast, and grumbled off to our rooms.

In the morning we stopped at the Hofwyl-Broadfield Plantation State Historic Site, which was reputed to be a wellspring of Painted Buntings. According to a park brochure, "This beautiful plantation represents the history and culture of Georgia's Rice Coast. The plantation and its inhabitants were part of the genteel, low-country society that developed during the antebellum period. While many factors made rice cultivation increasingly difficult in the years after the Civil War, the family continued to grow rice until 1913."

It was a lovely plantation with some spectacular big old trees, but it did not have the look of a world-class birding spot to us, so we turned up our noses and motored on. But before leaving we spent some time in the visitor center. The docent there told us that her mother had recently been a resident at a hospice for the terminally ill, and that there had been Painted Buntings in the vegetation and the feeders around this hospice. More about this hospice later.

Close by the plantation was the Ansley Hodges M.A.R.S.H. (Matching Aid to Restore States' Habitat) Project, also known as the Altamaha Wildlife Management Area. We drove into this area for several miles on dirt roads straining every nerve to see a bird of some kind. We also walked along a dike for several hundred yards but found only Red-winged Blackbirds, an Indigo Bunting, and miscellaneous other common birds. It *is* great Painted Bunting habitat. Just not for us.

Traveling north along the coast, our next stop was Harris Neck National Wildlife Refuge. This refuge is bounded on the north and east by the South Newport River and by Harris Neck Creek on the south side. It was famous during the late 1700s and early 1800s for the fine quality of Sea Island cotton that was grown on plantations covering the area. Part of the refuge had been an airfield and pilot training center during World War II. What with the surrounding water, numerous ponds, and considerable swampland, we were expecting great things from this refuge. It was ideal bird habitat. We took the Seven-Mile Drive, looking for anything, especially Painted Buntings.

What we found instead was a Wood Stork rookery.

We had seen Wood Storks the previous day, but finding this rookery had all of us excited. It was an amazing sight with the blue water, the green forest, the large dead trees, and storks all over the place.

The Wood Stork is a big, white, long-legged bird with black trailing edges to its wings. It has a dark neck and face, along with a huge ugly black beak. With a wingspan of five feet it is spectacular in flight. There were a great many of these storks flying and sitting around the rookery. Sharing that same area, numerous herons, egrets, and a few alligators were lurking around hoping some young bird would tumble from its nest into waiting jaws.

Next on our list for the day was Fort Morris State Historic Site, which sits on a low bluff on the Medway River. This fort was established to protect the town of Sunbury, which was a good-sized port before the Revolutionary War. It's located just south of Savannah. The British captured the fort and adjacent town during the war, and the place went into decline almost immediately.

The story goes that when the British first came to capture the fort, Col. John McIntosh replied, "Come and take it!" Only history knows whether he was being defiant or really wanted to get rid of the place. The tourist literature calls him defiant, and why wouldn't they? That's how I'd want to be remembered if I were him. At first, the British left, but later they came back and took him up on his offer.

The manager of the fort's visitor center noticed the physical condition of two of our group and kindly offered us a golf cart to get around the grounds. I was elected to drive and Lorraine, Irene, and Dorothy piled in. I took off, whizzed around what is left of the fortifications and then took a nature trail that, in retrospect, was never meant to be traveled any way but on foot. But once we started, I plowed ahead, bouncing over roots and rocks, with the three girls hanging on for dear life, giggling, and demanding to know if I had gone 'round the bend. I don't think they were referring to the curves in the trail. When I slowed almost to a stop in order to climb over a rather big root, Irene bailed out with some snide remark about her preference for walking no matter how excruciating it might be.

After a short stop at the Sunbury Cemetery, we drove back into Brunswick, where we hit the low point of our adventure. Remember the hospice for the terminally ill? The one with the Painted Buntings hanging around the bird feeders to ease the last days of the patients? We got it into our heads that maybe they wouldn't mind sharing their Painted Buntings with us.

We had no sooner pulled into the parking lot when Steve crawled under a seat and begged us to not tell them he was with us. I still have no idea why he thought he was unwelcome. Ted volunteered to go inside and ask permission to look around the grounds. He soon returned with what he said was a heartfelt "go for it." Several of us walked around, checking all the feeders and shrubbery, but we didn't see a single bird. Steve claimed it was cosmic payback for something. He never told us what.

On the way back to Embassy Suites in the Mall, we struggled once again with where to eat dinner. As you know, food is never far from being uppermost in the minds of this group. We all knew we didn't want to go anywhere near the Mall for food again, and no one felt like cruising the entire length of Brunswick in search of the perfect place. So I took the bull by the horns, willing to let the chips fall where they may. After all, when you're on the horned end of a bull, chips are at the far end of the problem, so to speak. I pulled into a place that said "Steakhouse" on it, shut off the van, and climbed out. The others meekly followed. It turned out to have some of the best food we had on the entire trip. For half a second I thought of taking credit for this, but I gave up after a few mumbled comments about how extraordinarily lucky I had been.

Sunday morning we were up and on the road by our usual 8:15. That late a start is almost blasphemy to a fanatical birder, but we didn't have any of those along.

Our first stop for the day was going to be Skidaway Island State Park. This is the place that had promised to have Painted Buntings waiting for us. Skidaway is an offshore island connected to the mainland by marshes, another small island, and a causeway. The park consists of 588 acres of both salt- and freshwater wetlands, part of it lies on the Intracoastal Waterway. It boasts nature trails which wend their way through marshes peppered with live oaks, cabbage-palmettos, and long-leaf piney woods. In other words, a great habitat for birds.

After checking out the feeders, we took a hike on a loop trail through the swamps and woods. It was a great place for birds, but the tide was not right, the light was all wrong, the time was off, and the cosmic payback thing must still have been in play because we saw nothing of any import. When we got back to the feeders, they were still empty.

Because we had the feeling this would be our last chance to see a Painted Bunting, we started out on the loop trail again. Suddenly Steve noticed a small bird sitting high up in a snag right between us and the sun. It could have been anything. Steve immediately pronounced it a Painted Bunting. Since there was no way to know for sure, we all readily agreed. Buoyed by this amazing discovery, Steve and Ken continued down the trail. But I decided to hang around the area for a while, and the others went back to sit and watch the feeders.

At some point in the past couple of days Dorothy had purchased a plush Painted Bunting toy for her granddaughter Caitlin. On our walk around this Skidaway Island swamp, Dorothy carried this toy along. Every once in a while she would give it a squeeze and it would emit the call of a Painted Bunting.

At one point she placed this replica on the bird feeders, and everyone took a picture to show that we actually knew what a Painted Bunting should look like. The coloring of this stuffed toy was quite accurate; and after all, it might be the only one we'd see.

At Last—the Elusive Painted Bunting!

No sooner had she done this than a real Painted Bunting flew in and landed on the feeder. They called me excitedly to join them, and we spent some delightful time watching this beautiful little jewel of a bird come and go. A Painted Bunting is really something to see with its brilliant patches of red, green, and blue. Eventually Ken and Steve came puffing out of the bushes claiming they had seen Painted Buntings all over the place on the other side of the swamp. At last we had met our goal!

With the exception of Lorraine and I, our whole group had been Painted Bunting virgins. Virgins no longer, everyone was happy and ready to move on.

Tybee Island

Skidaway Island is on the southeast side of Savannah; our next stop was Tybee Island, straight east of town. To get there, we had to go back into Savannah and then out toward the island. But before we could, the group demanded once again to be fed. After rejecting a couple of likely spots, we ended up at a Mexican eatery. The best thing I can say about it is that we ate what they brought us, determined to keep up our strength.

Tybee Island is billed as the best place in Georgia to find a Purple Sandpiper. Now there are 411 kinds of sandpipers, all smallish, brown/gray, pointy-billed, and skittering around like they're possessed. They all look alike. And the Purple Sandpiper has nothing purple about it. We knew this was going to be a challenge.

We found the spot and started looking. We saw pelicans, skimmers, and several other shore birds, but no sandpipers of any kind. But that was okay. Even with Steve's 40-power glasses, we would have been there the rest of the day trying to figure out which sandpiper was which.

Savannah

We had planned to make a couple of stops after Tybee Island, but no one had the heart for it, so we headed into Savannah. We were staying at the DoubleTree in Savannah's Historic District and wanted to take a look around if we ended up with some extra time. Once we got settled, we arranged for a trolley to pick us up and take us for a 90-minute tour around town. It was well worth the investment of a little money and time.

Savannah was settled in 1733 by General James Edward Oglethorpe and a little band of English settlers. The main thing that Oglethorpe gave to the future of Savannah was the manner in which he laid out the town. In the historic district there are about twenty-two squares situated in a symmetrical pattern, each taking up about one-half block. They are all the same size. Each is like a little park, with old, Spanish-moss-draped oak trees, flowers, and the occasional monument. These open squares are lined with stately old homes, churches, shops, and galleries.

Savannah was at the end of the line on General Sherman's devastating March to the Sea, but evidently he was tired of slashing and burning. He spared the city and gave it to Abraham Lincoln as a birthday present. The city has preserved a lot of really wonderful antebellum architecture.

For dinner Steve made reservations at a place called The Pirate's House. This restaurant is located in a big, old house about two blocks back from the riverfront. The lobby, to help entertain those who are waiting, sports a life-sized pirate figure who will tell a joke if you push his button.

When our table was ready, we were escorted through one dining room, around a corner, down a hall, around several corners, through several more rooms, down more halls, and then into a small room with just one big table. One more door and we would have been in the alley. We sat down, ordered our drinks and dinner, and then waited. While we waited, Steve noticed a fly in Ken's water glass. He took it away and got a replacement. Ken hadn't seen the fly. He had no idea what Steve was up to. When his new glass of water arrived, he made Irene take a sip to make sure that it wasn't really a cocktail. Evidently Irene is a cocktail expert of some repute. Why Ken thought Steve would sneak him a cocktail is probably a topic best left alone.

For some reason, that reminded Ted of the time he went in to get a hangnail checked and ended up with a colonoscopy. He was having a hard time getting over the end result (pun intended). That led to numerous suggestions from Ken and Steve on ways to automate and simplify the colonoscopy and other exams in that general region of the anatomy. By this time we were all laughing and hooting so hard and loud that we were glad they'd put us on the backside of beyond in a room by ourselves. I'm sure the management felt the same way. I just wonder how they they were able to tell what we were going to be like from the get-go.

Back at the hotel we sat in the lobby discussing the upcoming family reunion. We asked the hotel about breakfast...well, let me back up a minute. The other places we had stayed had complimentary breakfasts—pretty good ones in fact. So we checked with the hotel and found that they did indeed serve breakfast—for a price. Not that we're perverse, but if they were going to charge for breakfast we weren't having any of it. We decided to drive out of town a ways and get breakfast wherever we could find it. I guess we didn't stop to think we'd be paying for breakfast anyway.

The next morning on our way back to Atlanta, we stopped at a Huddle House to eat breakfast. I'd always wondered what those places were good for. The answer is "Pancakes!"

Until We Meet Again

In Atlanta we found the Airport Marriott via a new and interesting route and dropped off Ken, Irene, Ted, and Dorothy. Good driving weather made the trip home more pleasant than when we left. Steve helped out by reading his book about Captain Cook and napping. I didn't mind steering that clumsy little bus down the freeway at all. We dropped Steve off in London and drove home.

It was a good birding trip. We didn't see that many birds, and the birding locations mostly sucked, but being with the family made up for those deficiencies. We talked, laughed, embarrassed ourselves (well, we *should* have been embarrassed), and had a grand old time. And we finally reached our goal. We were Painted Bunting virgins no longer.

There were only a couple of times when my driving made the passengers review their past lives, so I must be getting better. And all the motels/hotels turned out to be rather okay, which was a new experience for us.

Here are the birds we saw, thought we saw, and maybe in a few cases, hoped we would see. Take your pick. We don't much care.

Birds we saw on the first day:

Killdeer, Wild Turkey, Green Heron, Great Blue Heron, Snowy Egret, Canada Goose, Turkey Vulture, European Starling, Northern Mockingbird, Brewer's Blackbird, and Great Egret.

New birds we saw on the second day:

American Crow, Philadelphia Vireo, Northern Parula, Nashville Warbler, Prothonotory Warbler, Gray Catbird, Anhinga, Red-shouldered Hawk, Cooper's Hawk, Cape May Warbler, Sandhill Crane, Osprey, Black-throated Green Warbler, White Ibis, Red-bellied Woodpecker, Black Vulture, Red-headed Woodpecker, Eastern Towhee, Common Nighthawk, Pileated Woodpecker, Eastern Kingbird, White Morph of a

Great Blue Heron (Great White Heron), and Red-cockaded Woodpecker.

New birds we saw on the third day:

Cattle Egret, Black-and-white Warbler, Common Yellowthroat, Summer Tanager, Blue-gray Gnatcatcher, Northern Cardinal, Brown Pelican, Red-winged Blackbird, Brown Thrasher, Eastern Bluebird, Downy Woodpecker, Carolina Chickadee, Black-throated Blue Warbler, Pine Warbler, Marbled Godwit, Willet, Boat-tailed Grackle, Ruby-throated Hummingbird, Wood Stork, Mourning Dove, Laughing Gull, Little Blue Heron, Mallard, Black Skimmer, Ruddy Turnstone, Caspian Tern, and Least Tern.

New birds we saw on the fourth day:

Indigo Bunting, Blue Grosbeak, Common Snipe, Purple Martin, Tree Swallow, Purple Gallinule, Common Moorhen, Brown-headed Cowbird, and Carolina Wren.

New birds we saw on the fifth day:

Wood Duck, White-breasted Nuthatch, **Painted Bunting**(!), and Double-crested Cormorant.

Afterword

Everyone defines fun in his or her own way, but for me and my family, fun is the result of getting together and spending time being ourselves. In our case, birding is our excuse. It must be true of other birders as well, for you seldom see a solitary birder. Usually they come in groups of two or more.

Most states and other countries have also recognized this phenomenon, which explains nearly every state's effort to attract birders. They want people to enjoy their territory and spend money while they're at it. The popularity of birding also explains the many commercial tours available in the United States and most foreign countries. For a price you can find a birding tour that will take you anyplace in the world at any level of luxury you require.

Birding combines the stealth and sneakiness of any hunt, but without the physical exertion of, for example, lugging a hindquarter of elk up the side of a steep canyon. It also combines the endurance and agility required by most sports, but without the unlimited hours of training it takes to be, say, an Olympic slalom skier. This opens the activity up to an unlimited number of participants.

Birding can be done in your backyard or in any exotic place you can reach. (By exotic I mean anyplace outside your backyard.)

My family usually looks for a locale which is convenient for all of us to reach. Economics can play a part in site selection as well. And that's the glory of birding—you can go as far or as near as economics or time allow.

As far as support for the birder—there is a plethora of birding magazines, as well as many birding clubs, all of which exist to help entertain and educate anyone with any level of interest in the sport.

The sport has its own method of scorekeeping—life lists.

And its heroes? The Big Year participants.

Expecting the Unexpected

The most exciting part for me is that anything can happen while birding. Here's a short example:

Driving down a dike road in Malheur National Wildlife Refuge in Eastern Oregon, I spotted a Great Blue Heron standing in a field beside the road. I slowed down to take a couple of pictures with my long lens and then slowly backed the car up until I was even with the bird.

The heron didn't move.

I eased out of the car, making sure not to slam the door and startle the bird. I crept toward the rear of the auto, easing around the back bumper, leading with my camera.

The heron still didn't move.

I continued around the car toward the edge of the road.

Still the bird didn't move a feather.

Slowly I crept into the field, snapping pictures all the way. I changed to my short lens and kept moving toward the bird. It remained completely still. As I advanced I suddenly realized something was wrong. Soon I was kneeling beside the heron, no longer interested in photography.

The reason for the heron's seeming tameness? A piece of plastic discarded by some careless soul had become jammed over the bird's lower beak, preventing it from clamping shut on anything edible. It couldn't eat. It was in danger of starving.

As gently as I could, I removed the plastic, releasing the bird's bill. Wishing it well, I headed back to the car while the heron slowly made its way toward a nearby pond on its long stilt legs. I drove away feeling happy and grateful that I'd been there to rescue a beautiful bird from an otherwise inevitable and appalling fate.

So, what's next for me and my family? We're busy planning and looking forward to our next birding adventure and many more to come, always aware that we may stumble upon an opportunity to make a difference even while we're having fun.

Appendix: Birds-sighted List

Where We Went

1. Southeastern Arizona
2. High Island and East Texas Coast
3. Cape May, New Jersey
4. Texas Coast and Rio Grande Valley
5. Costa Rica
6. Southeastern Arizona
7. Southern Georgia Coast

Birds We Saw

Acorn Woodpecker [1, 6]
Agami Heron (Chestnut-bellied) [5]
Albert's Towhee [6]
Alder Flycatcher [5]
Altamira Oriole [4]
Amazon Kingfisher [5]
American Avocet [2, 3, 4]
American Bittern [2]
American Black Duck [3]
American Coot [2, 4, 6]
American Crow [3, 4, 7]
American Goldfinch [3]
American Kestrel [4]
American Oystercatcher [2, 3]
American Pygmy Kingfisher [5]
American Redstart [2, 3, 5]
American Robin [3, 6]
Anhinga [2, 4, 5, 7]
Anna's Hummingbird [1, 6]

Baird's Trogon [5]
Bananaquit [5]
Band-tailed Pigeon [5]
Bank Swallow [5]
Bare-throated Tiger-Heron [5]
Bar-headed Goose [3]
Barn Swallow [2, 3, 5, 6]
Barred Antshrike [5]
Barred Woodcreeper [5]
Bay Wren [5]
Belted Kingfisher [2, 4]
Bewick's Wren [1]
Black Duck [2, 6]
Black Guan [5]
Black Hawk [6]
Black Phoebe [1, 5, 6]
Black Skimmer [2, 3, 4, 7]
Black Swift [5]
Black Vulture [4, 5, 7]
Black-and-white Warbler [2, 3, 5, 7]
Black-bellied Plover [3]
Black-bellied Whistling Duck [4, 6]
Black-cheeked Woodpecker [5]
Black-chinned Hummingbird [6]
Black-cowled Oriole [5]

Common Yellowthroat [1, 2, 3, 5, 6, 7]
Cooper's Hawk [7]
Coppery-headed Emerald [5]
Couch's Kingbird [4]
Crane Hawk [5]
Crested Caracara [4, 5]
Crested Guan [5]
Crimson-collared Tanager [5]
Crimson-fronted Parakeet [5]
Curve-billed Thrasher [6]

Dotted-winged Antwren [5]
Double-crested Cormorant [2, 3, 4, 6, 7]
Dowitcher [2, 3, 4]
Downy Woodpecker [2, 3, 7]
Dunlin [3]
Dusky Antbird [5]
Dusky-capped Flycatcher [5]

Eared Grebe [4]
Eastern Bluebird [3, 7]
Eastern Kingbird [2, 3, 4, 5, 7]
Eastern Meadowlark [2, 4, 5]
Eastern Phoebe [1]
Eastern Towhee [7]
Eastern Wood-Pewee [5]
Elegant Trogon [1, 6]
Elf Owl [1]
Emerald Toucanet [5]
European Starling [2, 4, 7]

Fiery-billed Aracari [5]
Flame-colored Tanager [6]
Fork-tailed Emerald [5]
Forster's Tern [4]
Fulvous Whistling Duck [2]

Gadwall [2, 3, 4]
Gambel's Quail [6]
Gila Woodpecker [1, 6]
Glossy Ibis [2, 3, 4]
Golden-bellied Flycatcher [5]
Golden-browed Chlorophonia [5]
Golden-crowned Kinglet [1]
Golden-crowned Sparrow [3]
Golden-fronted Woodpecker [4]
Golden-hooded Tanager [5]
Golden-olive Woodpecker [5]
Gray Catbird [2, 3, 7]
Gray Hawk [4, 5, 6]
Gray Vireo [1]
Gray-breasted Jay [1, 6]
Gray-breasted Wood-Wren [5]
Gray-crowned Yellowthroat [5]
Gray-headed Chachalaca [5]
Grayish Saltator [5]
Gray-rumped Swift [5]
Great Black-backed Gull [3]
Great Blue Heron [2, 3, 4, 5, 6, 7]
Great Crested Flycatcher [5]
Great Egret [3, 5, 7]
Great Kiskadee [4, 5]
Great Tinamou [5]
Greater Pewee [1]
Greater Roadrunner [4, 6]
Greater Yellowlegs [3]
Great-tailed Grackle [4, 5, 6]
Green Heron [3, 7]
Green Honeycreeper [5]
Green Jay [4]
Green Kingfisher [1, 5]
Green Violet-ear [5]
Green-and-rufous Kingfisher [5]
Green-backed Heron [2, 4, 5]
Green-breasted Mango [5]
Green-crowned Brilliant [5]
Greenish Elaenia [5]
Green-winged Teal [2]
Groove-billed Ani [5]

Harris's Hawk [4, 6]
Hepatic Tanager [1, 6]
Hermit Thrush [1]
Herring Gull [2, 3, 4]
Hoffmann's Woodpecker [5]
Hooded Oriole [4]

Hooded Warbler [2]
Horned Lark [4]
House Finch [3]
House Sparrow [2, 4, 6]
House Wren [1, 3, 5]

Inca Dove [2, 4. 5]
Indigo Bunting [2, 7]

Keel-billed Toucan [5]
Kentucky Warbler [2]
Killdeer [2, 3, 4, 6, 7]
King Rail [2, 3]

Ladder-backed Woodpecker [4]
Laughing Falcon [5]
Laughing Gull [2, 3, 4, 5, 7]
Lazuli Bunting [6]
Least Bittern [2]
Least Grebe [4]
Least Tern [2, 7]
Lesser Goldfinch [6]
Lesser Ground-Cuckoo [5]
Lesser Scaup [2, 4]
Lesser Yellowlegs [2, 4]
Little Blue Heron [2, 4, 5, 7]
Little Hermit [5]
Loggerhead Shrike [1, 2, 4]
Long-billed Curlew [2]
Long-billed Thrasher [4]
Long-tailed Hermit [5]
Long-tailed Manakin [5]
Long-tailed Tyrant [5]
Long-tailed Woodcreeper [5]
Louisiana Waterthrush [3]

Magenta-throated Woodstar [5]
Magnificent Frigatebird [5]
Magnificent Hummingbird [1, 6]
Mallard [3, 6, 7]
Mangrove Swallow [5]
Marbled Godwit [2, 7]
Marsh Wren [3]
Masked Bobwhite [6]
Masked Tityra [5]
Mealy Parrot [5]
Mexican Chickadee [1]
Mexican Crow [4]
Mexican Wild Turkey (Gould's) [6]
Mississippi Kite [5]
Montezuma Oropendola [5]
Mottled Duck [2, 4]
Mountain Elaenia [5]
Mountain Plover [4]
Mountain Robin [5]
Mourning Dove [2, 3, 4, 6, 7]
Mute Swan [3]

Nashville Warbler [4, 7]
Northern Beardless Tyrannulet [4]
Northern Cardinal [1, 2, 3, 4, 7]
Northern Harrier [2, 4]
Northern Jacana [5]
Northern Mockingbird [2, 3, 4, 6, 7]
Northern Oriole [1, 2, 5]
Northern Parula [3, 7]
Northern Shoveler [2, 4]
Northern Waterthrush [5]

Ochraceous Wren [5]
Olivaceous Cormorant [2, 5]
Olive-backed Euphonia [5]
Olive-crowned Yellowthroat [5]
Olive-striped Flycatcher [5]
Orange-bellied Trogon [5]
Orange-billed Nightingale-Thrush [5]
Orange-billed Sparrow [5]
Orange-chinned Parakeet [5]
Orange-collared Manakin [5]
Orange-crowned Warbler [4]
Orchard Oriole [2, 3]
Osprey [2, 3, 4, 5, 7]
Ovenbird [2, 3]

Painted Bunting [7]
Painted Redstart [1, 6]
Pale-billed Woodpecker [5]

Palm Tanager [5]
Pectoral Sandpiper [2]
Phainopepla [1, 6]
Philadelphia Vireo [7]
Pied-billed Grebe [2, 4]
Pileated Woodpecker [7]
Pine Warbler [7]
Piñon Jay [1]
Piping Plover [2]
Plain Chachalaca [4]
Prairie Warbler [3]
Prothonotary Warbler [2, 5, 7]
Purple Finch [6]
Purple Gallinule [2, 5, 7]
Purple Martin [2, 4, 5, 7]
Purple-crowned Fairy [5]
Purple-throated Fruitcrow [5]
Purple-throated Mountain-gem [5]
Pygmy Nuthatch [1]
Pyrrhuloxia [4, 6]

Red Knot [2, 3]
Red-bellied Woodpecker [3, 4, 7]
Red-billed Pigeon [5]
Red-breasted Merganser [3]
Red-breasted Nuthatch [1]
Red-cockaded Woodpecker [7]
Reddish Egret [2, 4]
Red-faced Spinetail [5]
Red-faced Warbler [6]
Redhead [6]
Red-headed Woodpecker [7]
Red-legged Honeycreeper [5]
Red-lored Parrot [5]
Red-necked Grebe [3]
Red-shouldered Hawk [7]
Red-tailed Hawk [6]
Red-winged Blackbird [2, 3, 4, 5, 6, 7]
Resplendent Quetzal [5]
Ring-billed Gull [2]
Ringed Kingfisher [5]
Riverside Wren [5]
Roadside Hawk [5]
Rock Dove [3. 4. 5. 6]
Rock Wren [6]
Roseate Spoonbill [2, 4]
Rose-breasted Grosbeak [2, 5]
Rose-throated Becard [1, 4, 5]
Rough-legged Hawk [3]
Royal Flycatcher [5]
Royal Tern [2, 4]
Ruby-throated Hummingbird [2, 7]
Ruddy Duck [4, 6]
Ruddy Ground Dove [5]
Ruddy Treerunner [5]
Ruddy Turnstone [2, 3, 4, 7]
Rufescent Tiger-Heron [5]
Rufous Motmot [5]
Rufous Piha [5]
Rufous-and-white Wren [5]
Rufous-capped Warbler [5]
Rufous-collared Sparrow [5]
Rufous-naped Wren [5]
Rufous-sided Towhee [1, 3]
Rufous-tailed Hummingbird [5]
Russet Antshrike [5]

Sanderling [2, 3]
Sandhill Crane [7]
Sandwich Tern [2, 4]
Say's Phoebe [6]
Scaled Quail [1]
Scaly-breasted Hummingbird [5]
Scarlet Macaw [5]
Scarlet Tanager [2, 5]
Scarlet-rumped Cacique [5]
Scarlet-rumped Tanager [5]
Scarlet-thighed Dacnis [5]
Scissor-tailed Flycatcher [2, 4]
Scott's Oriole [1]
Semipalmated Plover [2]
Short-billed Pigeon [5]
Slate-headed Tody-Flycatcher [5]
Slate-throated Redstart [5]
Slaty Antshrike [5]
Slaty Antwren [5]
Slaty-tailed Trogon [5]

Wood Stork [7]
Wood Thrush [2, 5]

Yellow Grosbeak [6]
Yellow Rail [2]
Yellow Warbler [1, 3, 5, 6]
Yellow-bellied Elaenia [5]
Yellow-breasted Chat [1, 6]
Yellow-crowned Euphonia [5]
Yellow-crowned Night-Heron [2]
Yellow-faced Grassquit [5]
Yellow-headed Caracara [5]
YellowishFlycatcher [5]
Yellow-rumped Warbler [2, 3]
Yellow-throated Euphonia [5]

Zone-tailed Hawk [6]